Inclusion in Further Education

FURTHER
EDUCATION

Inclusion in Further Education

Lydia Spenceley
Series Editor Susan Wallace

FURTHER EDUCATION

First published in 2014 by Critical Publishing Ltd

British Library Cataloguing in Publication Data
A CIP record for this book is available from the British Library

ISBN: 978-1-909682-05-4

This book is also available in the following ebook formats:

MOBI ISBN: 978-1-909682-06-1
EPUB ISBN: 978-1-909682-07-8
Adobe ebook ISBN: 978-1-909682-08-5

Cover and text design by Greensplash Limited
Project management by Out of House Publishing
Printed and bound in Great Britain by TJ International Ltd, Padstow, Cornwall

Critical Publishing
152 Chester Road
Northwich
CW8 4AL
www.criticalpublishing.com

Contents

Meet the author

Lydia Spenceley

I am the curriculum leader for teacher education programmes at Grantham College where I manage and contribute to a range of initial teacher education and Access programmes. My main areas of research interest are in inclusion, the development of teacher identity, special educational needs and visual research methodology. I have published papers on the development of identity, auto-ethnography, special needs and the problems encountered by 'beginning' educators in a Further Education setting. I have a broad range of experience in education and training, having previously worked in settings ranging from commercial training and training agencies to prison education, and most recently Further and Higher Education.

Meet the series editor

Susan Wallace

I am Emeritus Professor of Education at Nottingham Trent University where, for many years, part of my role was to support learning on the initial training courses for teachers in the Further Education sector. I taught in the sector myself for ten years, including on BTEC programmes and basic skills provision. My particular interest is in the motivation and behaviour of students in FE, and in mentoring and the ways in which a successful mentoring relationship can support personal and professional development. I have written a range of books, mainly aimed at teachers and student teachers in the sector; and I enjoy hearing readers' own stories of FE, whether it's by email or at speaking engagements and conferences.

1 Introduction

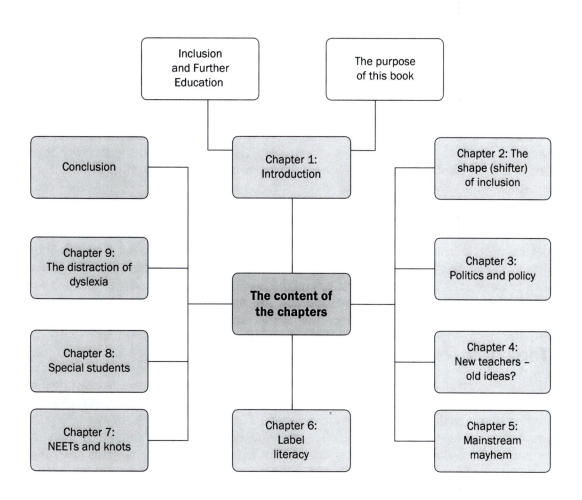

Chapter aims

This introduction explains the purpose of the book and provides a summary of the content, chapter by chapter. You may decide to read the chapters in order; but it might be that you need to select the chapter which will provide you with the information you are seeking in particular circumstances or at a specific time. Whichever approach you choose, these chapter summaries are designed to provide a helpful 'signpost' to the themes and arguments of the book as a whole.

Inclusion and Further Education

Wittgenstein (2011) in his *Tractatus Logico-Philosophicus* (Logical-Philosophical Treatise) argued that the limits of his language defined his world. In many respects our understanding of the term 'inclusion' defines the way that we implement the inclusive classroom practices that are now a requirement for those working as teachers, particularly those working in the varied context of Further Education (FE).

FE is characterised by many as one of the most inclusive providers of education due to the breadth and depth of the wide range of educational opportunities and qualifications it offers. But despite its willingness to work with students from all sections of society, Further Education remains one of the least known of the stars in the educational firmament. Few, until they enter its doors as teachers (or prospective teachers), realise the diversity of the sector and the commitment of the teachers within it to developing 'their' students, not just in an academic or vocational sense but as fully rounded young adults ready to take their place as fully functioning members of society.

In view of the diverse nature of the students that the sector invites into education or training, its ability to include them in the process of learning is critical to the success of both the individual and the sector itself. But the 'trick' of including them is one that has to be learned. This is particularly true for those who are relatively new or inexperienced teachers and who find the lack of definition of the term 'inclusion' (together with its proclivity to alter its meaning slightly from time to time!) disconcerting and unsettling.

The purpose of this book

This book is intended to help you if you are undertaking qualifications in teacher training or want to extend your knowledge of the subject with a critical understanding of the concept and its practical implementation in various settings. It does this by examining the interaction between the context (the classroom and workshops of FE) and the concept (the principle of inclusion) and by offering suggestions to develop inclusive practice. The range and variation of settings within FE is acknowledged and you are invited to critically engage with the prevailing policies and practice in those contexts through the use of 'real-life' case studies. In addition, you are invited to critically reflect on your own views and understanding of the concept of inclusion and the impact that it has on you as a teacher or trainee teacher and on your students, as well as on teaching and learning in general across the various FE settings.

The content of the chapters

Chapter 2: The shape (shifter) of inclusion

In *Alice's Adventures in Wonderland* (1865), Humpty Dumpty argues that he is the master of words, proposing that they mean what he chooses them to mean, neither more or less. Although Alice chooses to question this, he does have a point. Words change over time; their spelling and meaning are bound by their context, the intentions of the speaker and the agenda of the listener. The word 'inclusion' is no exception to this proposition and chapter 2 explores the changing use of the word in the shifting landscape of Further Education.

Based loosely on a historical timeline derived from Duke's (2009) work, the chapter considers how the definition of the term 'inclusion' has been interwoven with the notion of integration, in response to the norms, values and meta-narratives (the 'Big Stories' we collectively tell ourselves in the process of making sense of our world, such as that we are always progressing towards a better, fairer society) that currently predominate. The chapter challenges you to examine your understanding of the current influences on the meaning of the word 'inclusion', asking that you think about who and what is currently 'included' or 'excluded' by the current definition. Also addressed is the question of whether the attention of the FE sector is focused on working to include politically high-profile 'excluded' groups at the expense of tackling more deep-seated areas of inequality, as well as the debate over whether there are different *levels* of inclusion within FE. Through a discussion of Hodkinson's (1998) proposition that inclusion can be viewed as a continuum, we also look at the degree of inclusion which can be applied to particular groups of students who have recently been 'included' in some way within the remit of FE: NEET, ESOL and SEN students.

You are invited to reflect on the influence of various discourses, including discourses about deficiency, normativity and social justice and of their associated terminology, on society's understanding of inclusion. As Cather, in Turkington (1998), notes, *Give the people a new word ... [or in this case a new definition] ... and they think they have a new fact*. Moving on to the current situation in FE, the chapter looks at the impact that these discourses have had on teachers and students, and on teaching and learning, within the sector. In a concluding section we discuss the changing role of the sector and of those who work within it in relation to promoting inclusion.

Chapter 3: Politics and policy

Education, as a concept, shares with the notion of inclusion the honour of being something that is generally seen as a 'public good'. However, it also shares with it the rather more dubious distinction of being something of a political football, shaped and characterised by the prevailing political and social context. In an attempt to examine the pressures exerted on education by political, social and economic factors, our understanding of inclusion in FE is explored through a variety of various political (with a small 'p') contexts.

The chapter begins with a brief overview of the values and beliefs that underpin the actions and rhetoric of the major political parties in terms of social policy, education and inclusion, with a particular focus on policy since the Second World War. The changes to education and the influence of the introduction of the welfare state on the role of FE in the period of post-war reconstruction are initially examined. The impact of the harsh realities of economic, technological and social change is then surveyed so that you can gain an understanding of why the role of FE has been repeatedly reviewed. The repositioning of the sector, from being a tool for the implementation of social policy to one with increasing responsibility for supplying skilled labour to meet government economic policy, is then discussed in terms of the effect this has had on inclusion in FE.

We go on to look at the commercialisation of FE under successive Conservative administrations between 1979 and 1997. Here you are asked to consider the impact of the various discourses of vocationalism, competition, public accountability and the market on inclusive practice. In the penultimate section, the promise of a brighter future for FE generated by New Labour's enthusiastic use of the slogan of 'Education, Education, Education' is contrasted with the increasing dissonance between policy and rhetoric under successive New Labour governments. We look particularly at the growing contradiction between legislation for social inclusion and the retention and development of Conservative practices to control and monitor the sector. The concluding part of the chapter reviews the emerging policy of the Coalition government and the current and future impact of new financial policies of loans on the inclusion of students.

Chapter 4: New teachers – old ideas?

New teachers entering FE are often pursuing a second career. Having been successful in their first career many of them find that they wish to give something back to their chosen vocation, and being sufficiently skilled they want to pass their skills on to succeeding generations by teaching. As a result of this, many new educators undertaking their teaching qualifications are considerably more mature than those who intend to teach in compulsory education and they have vastly superior levels of life experience.

For the majority of trainee FE teachers it will have been some time since they last attended an educational establishment as a student. As a result they may have little knowledge or experience of some of the current philosophies of inclusive practice that govern relationships in the classroom. This means that when confronted with a class for the first time they may have to revert to their own experience to inform their practice. Perhaps this was true in your case.

The purpose of this chapter is to identify the key areas of challenge for new teachers; those which are specifically related to inclusive practice and, to a lesser degree, those which relate to the more general issue of professionalism. Through a case study approach you are encouraged to identify areas of concern and to focus on potential ways of meeting these challenges in three main areas: the process of learning, working in groups, and strategies for encouraging learning. By investigating the practice and attitudes of the case-study teacher, you will be able to think critically about practical methods of including students in the learning process, particularly those with high levels of need.

One of the most difficult aspects of any teacher's job is the part they play in helping students to develop their skills in learning so that they are transformed from dependent, needy students into the independent, self-directed students that are a joy to teach in FE. The chapter considers some of the problems that face young people in making this transition, together with the potential barriers which impede effective communication, and it suggests methods that the teacher may wish to employ in facilitating this process of change. The final section in this chapter looks at motivation for learning and examines the role of group work, active learning and peer interaction in promoting an inclusive working ethos in the classroom.

Chapter 5: Mainstream mayhem

Learning support has become an increasingly important consideration in the provision of inclusive learning since the publication of the Warnock Report in 1978 encouraged the inclusion of students with special needs into mainstream teaching. While the demand for learning support has increased, there is no settled role for the Learning Support Assistant (LSA) or agreement on the role that they should fulfil. Using a case study, the problems that this non-alignment of expectations can cause is one of the first points for discussion in this chapter before you are invited to examine your own practice in relation to working with LSAs.

The role of the LSA in relation to inclusion in the classroom is explored further in the next section, with the impact of various discourses (financial, academic, medical and social) being discussed. The chapter then goes on to examine the role of the LSA in addressing the inclusion agenda in the classroom through their potential to engage with students with empathy rather than at a purely academic level. It looks at the importance of their role as mediators in the classroom, able to 'translate' the teacher's intentions and the information to be learned, by developing alternative explanations suited to the needs of students.

One of the most important elements of the chapter is the discussion of different types of teacher/LSA relationships and the impact that they can have on the learning environment and on the students themselves. Two different models are introduced, the 'master–servant' relationship and the 'expert–novice' relationship. The expectations that the LSAs have of the relationships is covered in the last part of the chapter, which is based on the author's own research into this area. In the course of this research two significant concerns became evident: communication between the teacher and the LSA, and the degree of discretion used by the teacher in terms of students' behaviour. We look at how these two factors impact on the effectiveness of the LSA in facilitating the learning process and their role as a mediator between both the teacher and student, and between students.

Chapter 6: Label literacy

Labels are attached to everything and everyone; *good, pretty, helpful, awkward, argumentative*, all are labels which may be attached to an individual in one context or another. Society, however, tends to 'judge a book by its cover' and by reading or being aware of a label which is attached to someone there is a danger of that individual being prejudged by the expectations it raises. Labels can be internalised by the 'wearer' who frequently tries to live up (or down!) to society's expectations of them. A positive label may lead to a positive self-image and patterns of behaviour whereas the internalisation of a negative label may well lead to the opposite.

Labels in education are particularly dangerous. Most teachers have very little pre-knowledge of their students at their first meeting, and what they have been able to gain is likely to be in the form of a series of labels which will inform their subsequent relationship with the student. Within any class in FE there will be students who have been labelled in various ways. In this chapter the most common ones, 'SEN' and 'spikey profiles', are examined in more detail. One other, possibly unexpected, label is also explored in this chapter – that of 'Gifted and Talented' or 'More academically able' which, when applied to students in the wider vocational context of FE, can be seen to apply to a significant number of students. Although labels can influence the initial impressions of teachers, it is essential in the interests of inclusion that ways are found of ensuring not only that 'labelled' students are included in the learning process, but that their individual learning potential is maximised.

Through the use of case studies this chapter encourages you to apply your own knowledge and skills as a teacher to key situations. It looks at how educational theory can be applied in order to develop ways of including students with very different individual profiles in learning. The chapter also focuses on differentiating for accessibility. It discusses various elements of the teaching process and suggests how differentiation can be employed to meet the needs of students and help individuals to challenge the impact of incorrectly applied labels.

Chapter 7: NEETs and knots

The plight of young people who are now classified as NEETs (Not in Employment Education or Training) is once again becoming one of the significant political issues of the day. FE has been charged (as previously) with helping to reduce the number of young people in this category and has responded to the challenge with a number of different courses.

'NEETdom' has its own historical predecessors and the initial part of this chapter examines the background of NEETs in a historical context. It looks at the political influences that shaped the policies implemented to address concerns about youth unemployment and it explores the role previously held by FE in trying to include these students within education and eventually in society. You will be encouraged to draw upon your own experience or views of NEETs in order to identify the barriers to inclusion in education that are faced by young people in this group. The chapter considers ways in which these obstacles have been addressed previously and suggests areas that might need to be addressed in ways which have not previously been fully explored within FE.

Within the literature on NEETs there is considerable emphasis on the effect that a negative experience of education has had on students in this group. Duffy and Elwood (2013) identify four main categories of discontent associated with students' prior education, all of which focus on the difficulty experienced in developing and sustaining positive relationships with peers, teachers and the institution in the educational context. The chapter emphasises the need to understand the emotional context of learning and the importance of the enabling role of the teacher in using emotional intelligence to include this group and facilitate the building of constructive relationships. It discusses the potential application of the work of various writers on emotional intelligence and you will be asked to draw your own conclusions about the potential of these theories for developing NEET students' readiness to learn in the safety of an emotionally intelligent learning environment.

Chapter 8: Special students

This chapter looks at 'special students' who were 'included' in mainstream education after the Warnock Report (1978). Special students are those who have Moderate Learning Difficulties or Profound and Multiple Learning Difficulties. Their difficulties have made it impossible for them to be educated in mainstream school so they have been educated in schools that specialise in particular types of difficulty. Special students have been entering FE in increasing numbers in recent years and this chapter looks at the challenges their special needs present to teachers.

The chapter begins with a case study in which you are asked to think about the management of students within your own institution. It goes on to look at how the different ways of managing special students in FE can be explained at a theoretical level by applying some of the tools provided by Foucault and Bourdieu. By thinking about these different explanations you will be encouraged to reflect on how the management of special students can affect the way that they are included in the life of the college. One of the main aims of FE is to help students to develop and to prepare them to take their place in society and the world. Through a case study you are asked to think about whether FE is able to offer comparable opportunities to these special students and consider the steps that some institutions are taking to help to improve their ability to access society.

The last part of the chapter continues with the theme of the management of students; but in this section it is the role of the teacher which is examined. Again the 'tools' of Bourdieu and Foucault are used to analyse current practice and you are encouraged to think about whether the role of the teachers of special students is one of controlling or caring for the individual. Although the management of special students is fragmented, the chapter ends on a slightly more optimistic note, pointing out that a specific pathway for the training of new teachers who wish to specialise in working with special needs students has recently been introduced by the government.

Chapter 9: The distraction of dyslexia

Dyslexia is probably one of the most common of the Specific Learning Difficulties which you are likely to encounter in FE. It is thought that about 1 : 10 in the general population may have some form of dyslexia. However, my own experience of FE suggests that about 1 : 4 of students have reading difficulties, many of which can be associated with dyslexia. This means that whatever you teach and whatever level you teach at you are likely to have a student in your classroom with literacy difficulties. But most teachers, and this may include you, have not been trained in working with students with dyslexia.

Dyslexia is a very difficult condition to pin down as it affects people in very different ways. For some it may be difficulty reading the words themselves, whereas others might have difficulty understanding and remembering what they read. In a society that is 'literacy-centric' (very reliant on words and reading and writing for communication and education), students who experience difficulties with literacy or have dyslexia are at risk of being excluded from the full range of education. One of the purposes of this chapter is to explore ways in which you can help to include students in the learning process so that they can achieve their full potential.

At the moment the cause of dyslexia is unknown and so there is no certain 'cure' but this chapter gives you some information on the current theories that speculate on its cause. After looking at some of the possible causes, a case study encourages you to think about the different ways in which dyslexia is viewed from the point of view of (some!) teachers, dyslexic students and society itself. You are asked to take part in a critical thinking activity that explores the difficulties you might face when working with students who do not disclose their dyslexia. This activity sets the scene for a short analysis of the potential impact of dyslexia on teaching and learning.

Most people think of dyslexia as a difficulty in reading and writing. However, there is some evidence which suggests that it is a processing difficulty in the brain. This view might explain a form of dyslexia which we find quite often in FE where you may find that you are working with students who can read the words but have a problem with comprehension and understanding the meaning of text. Through the use of a case study you are asked to identify the difficulties that this may present to the student (and the teacher!) and to detect strategies that adult students may have developed to cope with this. The final element of the chapter makes some practical suggestions to help teachers include those with this form of difficulty in the mainstream classroom.

Conclusion

The intention in writing this book was to help you to critically assess and extend your knowledge of inclusion in different contexts through studying a series of case studies and carrying out critical thinking activities. In looking back over the chapters and taking part in the reflective activities you may have discovered a number of different threads that run throughout the text. Some of the threads are negative. For example, you might feel that government policy and its attempts to move FE from its post-war remit as a tool for inclusion and personal development to being a sector that is mainly concerned with preparing young people to work is unfortunate. However, although we have seen the role of FE become increasingly contested and contentious, the staff who work within FE have retained their commitment to the ethos of inclusion and to building a more inclusive society.

On a more positive note, you might have found it inspiring to see the different ways that FE uses communication. Not only do teachers communicate at different levels, but many teachers (and you may be one of them) have become very skilled in different ways of communicating, using speech, writing, transactional analysis, empathy and emotional intelligence to promote inclusion and learning. Another theme, although I don't think it is mentioned directly more than a couple of times, is the way that FE works to develop respect. First and foremost, FE respects the students, many of whom have had a poor experience of compulsory education. It takes considerable courage for these students to come back into education or to take on the challenge of a vocational course, particularly if they have been made to feel 'different' in some way. You and your colleagues work hard to give these students a good experience of education using activities that will interest and engage them in learning. But more importantly you also work with them in the affective domain to build the self-respect, self-esteem and self-confidence that is so frequently absent.

'Respect' to all of you; you've earned it!

References

Carroll, L (1865/2010) *Alice's Adventures in Wonderland*. Oxford: Oxford University Press.

Cather, W (1988) Four Letters: Escapism, in Turkington, C (ed) *The Quotable Woman*. New York: McGraw Hill.

Duffy, G and Elwood, J (2013) The perspectives of 'disengaged' students in the 14–19 phase on motivations and barriers to learning within the context of institutions and classrooms. *London Review of Education*, 11(2): 112–26.

Hodkinson, P (1998) Career Decision Making and the Transition from School to Work, in Grenfell, M and James, D (eds) *Bourdieu and Education: Acts of Practical Theory*. London: Falmer Press.

Wittgenstein, L (2011) *Tractatus Logico-Philosophicus*. Radford, VA: Wilder Publications.

Websites

Duke, Jennifer (2009) *Inclusive Education Discussion Paper*. (Unpublished) QUT Digital Repository: http://eprints.qut.edu.au/26314/1/c26314.pdf.

2 The shape (shifter) of inclusion

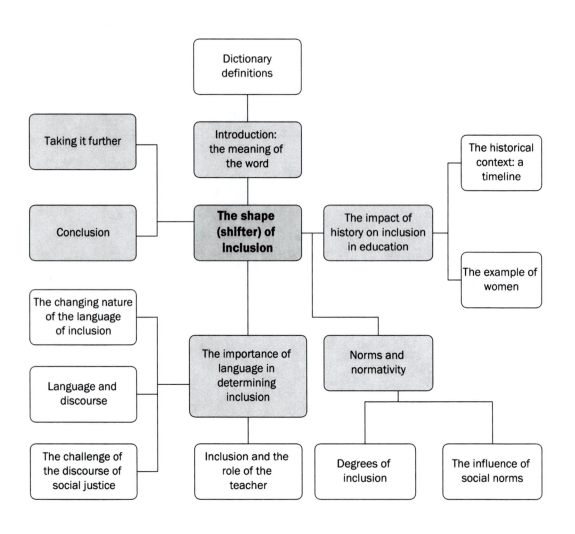

Chapter aims

Many of the terms we take for granted in teaching and learning are really quite complicated. Most of the time we use them without thinking and just assume that we are using the right word for the job. Inclusion is one of the words that is complicated, and the purpose of this chapter is to see how its meaning has changed over time, to look at the background to the changes of its meaning and to enable you to reflect on what you mean by inclusion.

Introduction: the meaning of the word

One of my 'best friends' over the years has been an old dictionary. Frequently it has been of help to me in clarifying the meaning of difficult or obscure words or in defining concepts concisely and precisely, and it has often acted as a mental launch pad when devising lessons or thinking about assignments. Having been packed and repacked innumerable times for job, office or home moves, it is now showing its age. The binding is battered and the pages dog-eared, but more importantly, although many of the words it contains are the same, over the years their definitions have subtly changed or been extended as language develops to reflect the society from which it stems. Sadly, its usefulness is now diminishing and my searches for meanings in its yellowing pages are frequently supplanted by a quick Google search or a dip into an online dictionary that contains more contemporary references.

'Inclusion', what a word! Together with its sister word 'differentiation' it is one that has become central to the vocabulary of all teachers. Bandied around recklessly in educational circles and wider society, it's one of those words that everyone knows and can define – or can they? Understanding terms and concepts is one of the keys for personal professional development for all reflective practitioners. Without an appreciation of the terminology itself, its roots, its political and social connotations and the significance of its use within a particular context, how can we judge impact on our personal professional practice?

Critical thinking activity: what does inclusion mean to you?

» *Before continuing with this chapter (and without resorting to a dictionary!) take a minute to write down your definition of the term 'inclusion'.*

Dictionary definitions

My old dictionary defines inclusion in several ways:

> *The act of including something; the condition of being included ... the body or particle distinct from the substance in which it is embedded*
> (*Concise Oxford Dictionary*, 1990: 687)

However, an online search adds to this list, informing me that its derivation is *from Latin inclusio(n-), from includere 'shut in'* (www.oxforddictionaries.com, 2013). The Collins

Dictionary (online, 2013), while acknowledging the elements articulated in the Oxford Dictionary, suggests that the word also has a mathematical meaning *being the relation between two sets that obtains when all the members of the first are members of the second* X⊆Y. This train of thought is added to by the Freedictionary (online, 2013), which adds a more contemporary, computer-based element to the definition, showing that the word can now also mean *a logical operation that assumes the second statement of a pair is true if the first one is true.*

There are similarities as well as differences between these definitions. You may have noted that each has the idea of borders which enclose or 'shut in' something. The second definition suggests that there is a relationship between the different parts but that it is based on power, with the powerful part able to accept the smaller groups on the basis of similarities between them. The third definition contains within it the unspoken idea that if one part of an equation is true then the second part must also be true. As equations can contain 'and' 'or' statements, then, if something is included, logically something else must exist beyond its boundaries and therefore be excluded. But what is it that must be excluded and why?

Critical thinking activity: included or excluded?

Throughout history there have been examples of inclusion and exclusion. Take a few moments to consider the notion of exclusion in terms of the history of education.

» *Write down any groups who have been excluded from education.*

» *Next, write down the reasons for their disqualification.*

The impact of history on inclusion in education

Your list might be quite long and the reasons for the exclusion of some groups from education quite complex. You may have included generic, but socially distinct, categories such as the poor, women, servants, slaves, or those distinguished by physical characteristics such as physical impairment or ethnicity. You might also have thought of those who have been excluded for less obvious reasons such as speakers of other languages, those who hold different religious beliefs or cultural values, and those who have a learning difficulty or mental impairment. All of these groups have at some point in the history of education been subject to exclusion from education, and sometimes from society itself, on the basis of an identifiable difference of some sort. Their exclusion reflects the values, beliefs or norms of the society that chose to exclude them. Whatever the context, to be included or excluded is a direct result of a decision having been made.

While we all accept that exclusion exists, its existence raises a number of questions. Who decides to include or exclude someone or something? What issues influence the decision-making? What mechanisms are used to maintain the boundaries between those who are included or excluded? What factors might be involved in breaking down the barriers and promoting inclusion? To begin to answer these questions it is necessary to look further into the term 'inclusion' itself, to move beyond the common perception of the term as a benign and fundamental 'good' in society, and identify, explore and if necessary challenge the assumptions on which its current meaning is based.

The historical context: a timeline

Historically, exclusion within education has been dealt with in different ways. In her discussion of the development of inclusive education, Duke (2009) traces a historical timeline of the development of the four main types of educational response to the excluded: ignoring, segregation, integration and inclusion, a general framework that can be applied to educational policy and practice in the UK.

Ignoring

Prior to the Industrial Revolution, education was a privilege enjoyed by the elite, restricted to the upper strata of society, after being liberated from the absolute dominion of the clergy in the Reformation of the sixteenth century. Basic education and literacy skills were not required by the majority of groups in a predominantly agrarian society who were powerless and consequently ignored. With the advent of the Industrial Revolution and the rise of what Marx described as the capitalist system in the late eighteenth and early nineteenth centuries, education was gradually extended to different groups. Basic education and literacy skills were introduced through various private initiatives which provided the rising middle classes with the skills required by the growing industrial society. The educational needs of the general population, who had no political, social or economic power, continued to be ignored. The only exception was for a small group of children who were forced into education under the auspices of various pieces of legislation such as the Factory Acts, the Reformatory and Industrial Schools Acts and the Poor Law Acts in an attempt to equip them for employment.

Segregation

In the late nineteenth century's growing economy there was an increasing demand for a workforce with general literacy skills, and, in response to this, Forster's Education Act (in 1870) introduced a system of elementary education for the general population. Although you could argue that education became more inclusive following the 1880 Education Act, which made attendance at school compulsory until the age of ten, and the 1891 Education Act, under which elementary education effectively became free, it was in fact a segregated and segregating system. Education, other than the purely functional elements of the '3 Rs', remained largely the province of those who could afford it beyond the mandatory school-leaving age, which excluded the general population. For a few exceptional students, scholarships to grammar schools allowed them to remain in education. However, as uniforms, books, paper, pens, etc. all had to be paid for, few of the general populace could remain in education even with scholarships.

Integration

Between the World Wars there was a general growth in secondary education due to the raising of the school-leaving age. The next major change, and one with which you are probably familiar, was Butler's 1944 Education Act. The intention of the Act was to challenge the status quo by providing children with forms of secondary education best suited to their abilities and aptitudes. Through the introduction of a tripartite system of education consisting of grammar schools for the teaching of academic subjects, secondary modern schools for more practical subjects and technical schools for those with mechanical, scientific or engineering ability, it was intended that everyone would be able to access appropriate education. However, children were effectively segregated at the age of 11 by being allocated to different regimes on the basis of their results in a selective test which became known as the eleven-plus.

Inclusion

The system of segregated schooling founded on selective testing based on 'intelligence' was eventually challenged by the introduction of the Comprehensive system in the 1960s. Comprehensive education attempted to combine the different types of education into a single unified system that would allow students to be educated according to their ability in a single large, local institution. Although this system was primarily one of integration based on location, students' needs were increasingly catered for on an inclusive basis. New exams were introduced in 1986 (GCSEs, which replaced the dual system of GCE and CSE examinations), and course work rather than just closed examinations was considered as part of the overall assessment regime in an effort to make the system more accessible and fair. A new and universal National Curriculum was introduced in 1988 which was applied to all students. Students with specific needs were also gradually incorporated into the mainstream system following the Warnock Report of 1978 and the recognition of the rights of all students to formal education following the Salamanca Statement of 1994.

Critical thinking activity: the impact of context on the development of inclusive education

» *Using the timeline and the information above, think about how the education system reflected society during various periods in history.*

» *Consider the values prevalent in society during the different periods.*

» *Try to identify any social and political events that might have influenced the movement from ignoring, to segregation, through integration to inclusion.*

As you have gone through this thinking process you will have noticed the connection between events (both social and political) and the changes in society that have generated change within the education system. In the history of education there are obvious examples of significant groups within society being excluded from all or part of the education system.

The example of women

If we use Duke's (2009) analysis to look at the place of women in education, you will see the way in which changing social and political influences have affected their position in education. The educational needs of women were largely ignored by Victorian society who saw their primary role as that of parent or menial worker, which did not require education. Women were not admitted to universities until the 1870s and the few who were able to afford to attend were segregated. Women were forced either to attend all female Colleges such as Girton (founded in 1870 although its right to confer academic awards was not recognised at that time), or to attend lectures in a limited range of subjects deemed suitable for women at the few universities who would accept them. However, they were unable to obtain a degree. Following the First World War and the integration of women into the workplace, together with their eventual political emancipation in 1928, women gradually filtered into the Higher Education and the university system. It was not until the rise of the red-brick universities and the introduction of universal tuition grants in the 1960s that women became fully included in the education system. The same type of analysis can be made of other groups (ethnic minorities, those with different cultural or religious values, and those with learning differences) in terms of their journey from being ignored, through segregation and integration before becoming included in the education system.

Norms and normativity

As you will have seen from the example of women in education, all societies are affected by external conditions that give rise to social change. Historically, British society has been affected by momentous economic changes, for example:

• the rise of the industrial society and the influence of technology;

• major political events such as the First World War, the women's suffrage movement and feminism;

• social changes such as the increasing ethnic and cultural diversity within society; and

• the rise of new meta-narratives (the 'Big Stories' that influence society) of equality, social justice, individual rights and inclusion.

These meta-narratives influence the discourses (the ways of expressing fundamental beliefs or principles, so for example *equality* is a discourse, as is *liberty* or *freedom*). These in turn affect the norms (what people see as being normal or abnormal) of society, which are the basis that people use to make judgements about who should be included or excluded from society. Through the influence of norms not only do individuals and groups of people become visible or invisible, but their status as either included or excluded components of the social order becomes uncritically accepted.

The influence of social norms

Norms determine what is seen as normal and abnormal, and as such they are the frames of reference against which individuals and groups can be measured and any differences can be labelled as 'abnormalities'. Those who are seen as being 'normal' are accepted by society, but those who do not conform to the taken-for-granted standards of the norm become increasingly marginalised and powerless. Norms and discourses are constructed by society and are based on the social, cultural, political, physical or other characteristics that are specific to the group which is most powerful.

Norms are not written down and are in fact illusions; but they are tremendously powerful. They govern what people see as normal. So within your school or college it might be normal for students to dress smartly, or for all those in a particular vocational area to wear a uniform. In my own college it is normal to see all those who are studying for the Public

Services qualifications in a military-style uniform whereas those studying for catering quali-fications wear 'whites'. I'm sure you can think of other examples from your own experience. The problem comes when individuals don't conform to the normative ideal. Staying with the Public Services example for a moment, they all have bright, shiny, well-polished boots. A member of the class who turned up for the morning parade in dirty boots would be seen as non-normative and they would be punished in some way. In society it is the norm that chil-dren attend school. Traveller families who often withdraw their children from state education before the official school-leaving age are seen as non-normative and the traveller children become increasingly marginalised by mainstream society. As a group, travellers are seen as 'different' and non-normative as they do not live in a 'normal' home. Within their society to travel is seen as the norm, which shows that norms are determined by their context and are not fixed or stable, but will change with the society. Again, I'm sure that you can think of other examples from your own experience.

Critical thinking activity: who's included now?

Think about the current discourses and norms affecting inclusion in education.

» *What are the current 'hot spots' in terms of groups who, having been segregated in some way within the education system, are now being actively included?*

» *What are the assumptions that have underpinned their exclusion or segregation?*

» *Are these assumptions masking other more deeply ingrained social norms?*

You may have included on your list groups such as NEETs (those not in employment, educa-tion or training), speakers of other languages or those with special educational needs (SEN). You may also have decided that the current agenda to include these groups in education stems from a need for them to gain enough human capital (skills, knowledge, attitudes and values) to be assimilated into mainstream society and become active members of the com-munity. But have you thought about whether the discourses that affect the way you think and the norms that exist in society are focusing your attention on these groups at the expense of others? Is the current focus on including NEETs and SEN in FE diverting your attention from some of the more covert norms in society such as the *taken-for-granted nature of whiteness, and ablebodiedness and ability* in modern society noted by Graham and Slee (2006)? Now re-read the critical thinking activity above and think about your answers. Have they changed at all?

Degrees of inclusion

Many writers on the subject of inclusion (for example, Paliokosta and Blandford, 2010; Skidmore, 2004) suggest that an inclusive education system has the potential to challenge the norms in society which exclude certain groups. You may think that FE is an ideal candi-date for this role as it caters for a wide spectrum of society and offers a tremendous range of opportunities.

However, you might also want to argue that the process of inclusion in education is incom-plete as our efforts towards inclusion are focused on the obvious normative differences identified by society (NEETs, SEN, etc.) rather than those which are less obvious because they are more entrenched. If you are adopting this view then you might feel that FE is a tool to promote conformity. It recognises difference but, being funded to support the needs of specific groups (ESOL or SEN students), it also subtly suppresses underlying issues such as sexuality or gender.

Inclusion, like most things, is a process that takes time and Hodkinson (2012) identifies three major stages in the development of inclusive practice within education: *being* inclusive, *becoming* inclusive and to have *become* inclusive.

Being inclusive

In *being* inclusive the identifiable difference is seen as something that is part of the individual or group (skin colour, for example). Inclusion in this view is seen as a process of adaptation in which the 'different' person or group has to change or be changed in order to be accepted into the host society. An example of this might be the way that FE runs ESOL classes to help second-language speakers to understand English so they can access mainstream education.

Becoming inclusive

In the process of *becoming* inclusive the identified difference is perceived in more social terms; society itself makes some changes in order to include those who it perceives to be different in some way so that they can be functionally integrated into society. An example of this might be the changes made to schools and colleges to enable wheelchair users to access education, or LSA support supplied to students with literacy or behavioural difficulties. An illusion of inclusion is created as those who were excluded are accepted by the host society on the basis of the similarities between them, but the differences that excluded them in the first place (such as SEN or physical difficulties) continue to be labelled and made obvious to other members of society.

Become inclusive

The final form of inclusion identified by Hodkinson is that of having *become* inclusive. In this view inclusion is seen as being an interactive, empathic concept based on respect for all groups and individuals, in which there is a two-way relationship between the included and excluded. This enables all students to become part of a learning community in which the education system works with individuals to meet their requirements on the basis of individual need. In my college, the Learning Support specialist who works specifically with students who need some help initially in organising their work and structuring their assignments might be an example of this. Well, the title of this chapter is The shape (shifter) of inclusion, and as you can see it can be interpreted in a number of ways!

Critical thinking activity: being, becoming or become?

At the time of writing, each of the groups mentioned above (NEETs, ESOL students and those with SEN) receive some form of additional support in terms of education.

Consider their position in terms of the continuum of being included, becoming included or having become included.

»   *Is their position on this continuum one that varies according to context?*

»   *Are these groups at the same place on the continuum when viewed from the position of the educator and the institution?*

»   *If you think they are in different places, what are the contradictions that may arise?*

»   *What might be the impact on the teaching and learning process for members of these groups?*

In doing this exercise you may well have found that you feel that these groups are at different places in terms of inclusion. You may also feel that the position of some students or groups (SEN students, for example) may vary in the classroom, with some teachers, *being* inclusive while others have *become* inclusive in their practice. In thinking about other teachers, you may also see their pedagogic practices as *being* inclusive while they would see themselves as having reached the stage of having *become* inclusive. One of the ways that you may have identified these differences is through the language that is used both on behalf of the institution and also by the educators themselves.

The importance of language in determining inclusion

The changing nature of the language of inclusion

Language not only facilitates communication between members of defined groups – teachers or medical practitioners, for example – but it also contains symbolic power. Labels that indicate difference can be given to individuals or groups and each label contains society's view of the group or individual. When we 'read' the label it can subtly and subconsciously change our understanding of the nature of groups or individuals. For example, members of the traveller community might be described as gypsies, a word that attracts negative connotations and whose use affects the way in which this group is seen by society.

However, language is not static. In its role of reflecting and maintaining the norms and values of society, it also acts to incorporate and ameliorate the threat from new vocabulary that might present a challenge to these norms and values. The term 'inclusion' has the potential to be transformative as it suggests it is a mechanism for promoting participation and equality within society. To defuse this challenge to the status quo the term was absorbed into the vocabulary of education during the introduction of the Comprehensive system and its meaning subtly changed. This redefinition allowed it to describe the system of integration based on the physical location of students as being 'inclusive'. Over time its meaning has changed again and it is now used to describe strategies for responding to the needs and rights of the individual. As we saw at the beginning of this chapter, the term 'inclusion' is one that can be defined according to the context in which it is used. This situation may explain why you interpret some pedagogic practices as *being* inclusive while others see them from the point of view of having *become* inclusive.

Critical thinking activity: terminology, inclusion and Further Education

The terminology used within FE, and by FE educators, both reflects and contains within it the prevailing norms, values and meta-narratives of society.

» *Think about the language of inclusion that we use today – 'differentiation', for example. Make a list of words that you use (or have come across in your reading) that are associated with inclusion or inclusive practice in the classroom now.*

Language and discourse

When you were thinking about educational terminology for this exercise you probably noted down several terms that are in current use; for example, differentiation, special needs, whole class teaching, vulnerable students, fragile identities, at risk, disengaged, disaffected, etc. You may also have noted down a number of terms that were once current but are no longer used and are now seen as being discriminatory. These include terms such as ESN (educationally subnormal), imbecile, handicapped, retarded, etc. Underpinning the timeline model are two significant discourses: deficiency (which is about people having a lack or deficit of ability) and normativity (which is about what society accepts as 'normal'). The discourse of deficiency is principally (but not exclusively) associated with the periods of ignoring and segregation, whereas the discourse of normativity is generally linked with the periods of integration and inclusion. A third and equally powerful discourse, that of social justice, has recently made a contribution to the language used to describe inclusion and inclusive practice and is mainly associated with the last period – that of inclusion itself.

The discourse of deficiency

The discourse of deficiency is loosely based on the idea that it is the physical or mental part of the individual which is lacking and therefore different. As the difference or deficit is inherent within the individual it is not an issue or concern for anyone other than the individual. This model is also described as a medical model because individual difference can be seen as a sign of disease or deficiency. Those with medical differences may be feared or shunned by society. For example, historically those with a disease or a defect were disregarded by society in the 1600s, and in Victorian times they were seen as being in need of some form of special treatment and were segregated in asylums, prisons or hospitals. The language associated with this discourse reflects the view that the difficulty is a personal deficit, an 'abnormality' that might be 'curable' through 'interventions' following 'measurement' and 'diagnosis' designed to enable 'sufferers' of difference to change so that they conform to the expectations of society.

The discourse of normativity

The discourse of normativity, by comparison, is not based upon a need for an individual to conform to society but is based on the idea that society should accept individual difference as an essential part of the human condition and interact positively with those with difficulties. Individual difference is seen as a social problem that requires changes to be made in the prevailing norms to enable everyone to access society as a valued and product-ive member. An example of this might be the inclusion in mainstream FE of those with SEN or physical difficulties. Although individual difficulties are still identified, the stigma of diffe-rence is lessened through 'differentiation' to meet individual need in a society that embraces difference of all types. You may well be able to think of other words that are used to include in FE the students with differences.

The challenge of the discourse of social justice

The twentieth century was a time of immense change both nationally and internationally, with the demise of the colonial systems which had dominated the nineteenth century and the introduction of looser federations of states such as the Commonwealth. Political relation-ships between countries changed with the growing independence of the new nation states, although it could be argued that the colonial relationships were (at least initially) retained through the economic and trading relationships which continued. At the same time as demands for political freedom were made by the colonies, there was a growing awareness of the rights of the individual and the need to protect individual freedoms. These demands are perhaps best exemplified in the rise of the Civil Rights movement in the USA in the 1960s, with its pressure to end segregation and the repression of individual rights on the basis of colour.

From 'needs' to 'rights'

The growing demand for social justice, which is defined by the Oxford Dictionary (online, 2013) as being *justice in terms of the distribution of wealth, opportunities, and privileges within a society*, has been influential in shaping the current education system. The Comprehensive system, together with a raft of social reforms in the UK which addressed underlying social inequalities such as the Equal Pay Act 1970 and the Race Discrimination Act 1976, show its importance. Further developments such as the Warnock Report (1978) radically changed the idea of special educational needs within education, and the power of education as a transformative tool in society was recognised in the Salamanca Statement (1994) which affirmed, Europe-wide, the necessity for 'Education for All' in the construction of an inclusive society. Additional legislation such as the Disability Discrimination Act 1995, the Special Educational Needs and Disability Act 2001 and the Equality Act 2010 have maintained the pressure for inclusion within education.

As you will have noticed, the type of legislation recently introduced shows the increasing importance of inclusion in the latter part of the twentieth century and the first part of the twenty-first century and the emphasis on social reform. Legislation was introduced to match the need for social transformation in the move from a needs-based society to a rights-based society with emphasis placed not only on the rights of the individual but also on the citizen-ship agenda designed to facilitate social inclusion. Under this agenda education has increas-ingly become a site for the generation of social change, with FE in line with other areas of education moving from a needs-based education system to one based on rights.

Critical thinking activity: the impact of discourse on teaching and learning

»   *How do you think the different models might affect teaching in FE?*

»   *Make a few notes on how you think the different models have impacted on both teachers and students.*

Inclusion and the role of the teacher

As your notes will undoubtedly show, the role of the teacher in FE has changed significantly over the past few years. Your task is now to include your students by engaging them in the learning process, to inform, assess, and motivate and guide students in ways that, as Robson (1998) notes, overlap with the roles and responsibilities of other educational professionals such as librarians and counsellors. You are now expected to differentiate to enable your students to access the learning process as a matter of routine and by so doing you reflect and model the inclusive ethos of modern society. Inclusive teaching practices are common within FE; diversity is celebrated and the rights of young people to build and develop their social, cultural and economic capital are recognised in an atmosphere of unconditional positive regard (Rogers, 1961). However, you may have also noted that the administrative needs of 'the system' continue to demand that teachers and college administrators alike identify and label difference in order to access funding to make provision for additional support to meet individual need. While support may be seen as a means of developing opportunities to include all students in mainstream FE, it can also be seen as a part of the notion that everyone needs to be able to conform to the prevailing social norms of society.

More questions than answers?

The notion of inclusion is a transient concept, moving and reforming itself to match the changing pressures within society and it is one that, when examined closely, seems to raise more questions than answers for the teacher in FE. By supporting students in the classroom (including differentiation) and enabling students with challenging needs to conform to the mythical norm of the ideal student, is their need confirmed and made visible to all? On this basis are students with challenges really included within the education system or simply integrated? Students in FE have the right to refuse support, but does their refusal in itself mark them as being deviant in some way?

Other students with needs which preclude their inclusion in mainstream education, those with profound and multiple learning difficulties for example, are increasingly being located within FE colleges. Technically included within the mainstream system due to their relocation in the shared social space of colleges and the current requirement for them to be working towards qualifications, in reality, do their specific needs mean that they are effectively segregated within what is seen as an inclusive environment? Is what we describe as inclusion in education simply a blurring of the margins between inclusion and exclusion, or a real attempt to transform society?

Conclusion

If you have been a teacher in FE for a few years you will have seen changes in the range of students who now enter FE. With the rapid and continuing development of (increasingly affordable) forms of assistive technology, students who face physical or learning difficulties are now being more effectively included within mainstream provision. Other areas within the educational provision have also responded to the increasing influence of a social rather than the medical model of inclusion. Groups that have previously been seen as socially disadvantaged and educated under a segregated provision designed to promote skills facilitating social inclusion through gaining work, such as the Youth Training provision of the 1980s and 1990s, have been replaced by programmes for NEETs students within colleges. Students with behavioural issues that affect their learning and other groups that face challenges, for example, those with ADHD, autism or profound or multiple learning difficulties, now frequently form part of the overall community of students in an FE environment. On the face of it FE seems to be a highly inclusive part of the education system.

However, as the title of this chapter indicates, the term 'inclusion' is difficult to define without examining the context in which it is used. Although it is a commonly used word in FE (and society in general) it has been constantly and consistently redefined, and busy teachers like you rarely have time to think about its deeper meaning in terms of the way that the different interpretations affect individual students. It is a word that demands respect and is not one to be used lightly or without thought.

Chapter reflections

» *The term 'inclusion' is a slippery concept whose definition is influenced by the historical context in which it is used.*

» *The concept of inclusion is structured by the prevailing norms within a society.*

» *Those in power can direct the gaze of 'inclusion' away from underlying inequality towards areas that are more visible (although no less important!).*

» *Language is key in maintaining the prevailing and challenging discourses of inclusion.*

» *The role of the teacher and of FE in inclusion is both contested and contentious.*

Taking it further

Duke, Jennifer (2009) *Inclusive Education Discussion Paper.* (Unpublished) QUT Digital Repository: http://eprints.qut.edu.au/26314/1/c26314.pdf.

An interesting and informative view of the development of inclusive practice.

Kavale, K A and Forness, S R (2000) What Definitions of Learning Disability Say and Don't Say: A Critical Analysis. *Journal of Learning Disabilities*, 33: 239–56.

A useful look at definitions of disability.

References

Florian, L (2008) INCLUSION: Special or Inclusive Education: Future Trends. *British Journal of Special Education*, 35(4): 202–08.

Graham, L J and Slee, R (2006) Inclusion? In AERA 2006 Conference Proceedings, San Francisco CA 7–11 April 2006.

Hodkinson, A (2012) Illusionary Inclusion – What Went Wrong with New Labour's Landmark Educational Policy? *British Journal of Special Education*, 39(1): 4–11.

Kavale, K A and Forness, S R (2000) What Definitions of Learning Disability Say and Don't Say: A Critical Analysis. *Journal of Learning Disabilities*, 33: 239–56.

Paliokosta, P and Blandford, S (2010) Inclusion in School: a Policy, Ideology or Lived Experience? Similar Findings in Diverse School Cultures. *Support for Learning*, 25(4): 179–86.

Robson, J (1998) A Profession in Crisis: Status, Culture and Identity in the Further Education College. *Journal of Vocational Education and Training*, 50(4): 585–607.

Rogers, C (1961) *On Becoming a Person*. Boston: Houghton Mifflin.

Rorty, R (1989) *Contingency, Irony and Solidarity*. Cambridge: Cambridge University Press.

Skidmore, D (2004), *Inclusion: The Dynamic Of School Development*. Maidenhead: Open University Press.

Websites

Collins Dictionary online (2013). Available at www.collinsdictionary.com.

Duke, Jennifer (2009) *Inclusive Education Discussion Paper*. (Unpublished) QUT Digital Repository: http://eprints.qut.edu.au/26314/1/c26314.pdf.

Freedictionary online (2013). Available at www.thefreedictionary.com.

Oxford Dictionary online (2013). Available at www.oxforddictionaries.com.

3 Politics and policy

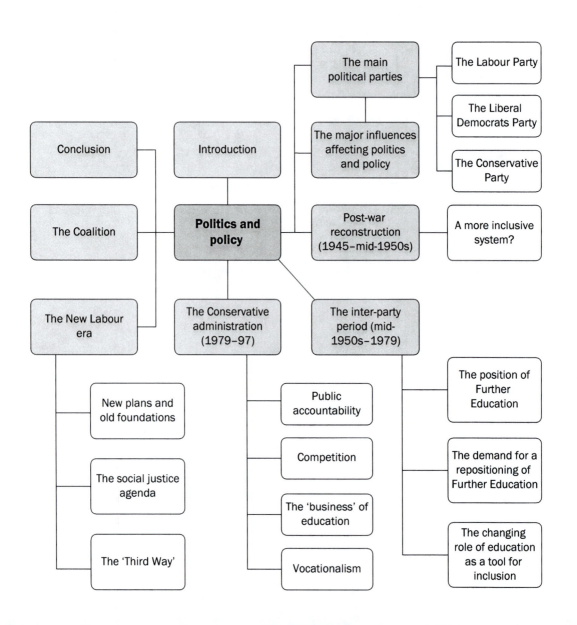

Chapter aims

This is the most unusual chapter in this book. Its purpose is to give you a historical overview of how politics and policy have affected the work of FE in contributing to building an inclusive society since the Second World War. The remaining chapters include case studies which you are encouraged to work through, but as this is a foundation chapter you are encouraged to participate and reflect through a series of critical thinking activities instead. The critical thinking activities will help you to examine the values and perceptions of the political parties which influence their attitude to FE and inclusion; to understand the pressures exerted on FE by the political context of the time and think about the tensions between FE as a business and government policy.

Introduction

The exact nature, purpose and content of education has always been an area of debate. You may think that its main purpose is to pass on knowledge and skills from one generation to the next, or to prepare young people for future jobs. But there is a wider dimension to education in any society as it is also a process of socialisation. It teaches young people about society itself and its values, beliefs and norms. As one of the key elements of secondary socialisation, the education system is of immense importance to society. The state has effectively controlled the education system in Britain, and educational policy and practice cannot be examined without taking into account the political context. However, you should note that there are variations between the English, Scottish, Welsh and Northern Irish contexts.

Within the UK system of government a number of political parties with different philosophical foundations compete for power and there is an ongoing debate about the future of education. This has resulted in education policy being in an almost permanent state of flux, subject to rafts of changes and propelled by the tides of reforms introduced by successive governments. As Shaull (1966) said in his foreword to Freire's *Pedagogy of the Oppressed [t]here is no such thing as a neutral educational process.*

Each administration is elected on the basis of policies that stem from their core ideologies or belief systems. In chapter 2 we looked at the development of inclusion using a historical continuum. In this chapter you will be using a slightly different type of continuum. Instead of being based on different understandings of inclusion, this one looks at political beliefs. Bartlett and Burton (2012) suggest that political beliefs extend from communism on the extreme left of the continuum to fascism on the extreme right, and this would place the major parties in British politics in a cluster around its midpoint. However, there are significant ideological differences between these parties and you will need to have some understanding of the main beliefs that influence the policies of the different parties before you can investigate their impact on educational policy and inclusive practices.

The main political parties

Critical thinking activity: what influences the influential?

» Make a list of the main parties who have been in power in the UK since the Second World War.

» Identify as many of their aims or values as you can.

» How do you think their aims and values affect their views on education, inclusion and their social policies?

You may have surprised yourself by finding out how much you know already about the political parties in the UK. You may have identified differences in terms of their views on the level of state control in society, the importance of individual agency (free will and the power to make decisions), the responsibilities of the individual to the state and the responsibilities of the state to the individual. All of these could influence their policies. It is not essential for you to know all of the details about the beliefs of each party, but you will need to have a general understanding in order to make sense of the impact of their policies. To help guide you through this chapter you will first read a broad-brush description of the belief systems that underpin their social policies and influence their policies on education and inclusion. In crude terms, a dividing line can be drawn between the beliefs and values of the Labour Party on the left and the Conservative Party on the right of the central point on the continuum. However, the ideology and beliefs of the main parties is not something that is fixed. Each party is a combination of factions with different beliefs which, at different times, influence the main views held by the party and which can influence their policies on education and inclusion.

The Labour Party

The Labour Party contains a number of different factions, and for the purposes of this overview they have been grouped together under two main headings: socialist and social democratic.

Socialist beliefs

The main beliefs of the socialist element come from the tenets of the early trade union movement and they emphasise the importance of collective action and the role of the state in eliminating inequality and unfairness in society. Their belief is that in a command economy the state would control the means of production (how things are produced, in factories, etc.) and the amount of goods produced to ensure full employment. Any profits would be used by the state to meet the needs of the individual in terms of housing, education, healthcare, etc.

Social democratic beliefs

Somewhat to the right of the socialists (although still on the left of the centre point of the main continuum) is the social democratic view. Like the socialists their philosophy is based on the principles of fairness and equality of opportunity, and like the socialists they believe that the state should meet the needs of individuals through the provision of key services. However, the social democratic view also recognises the existence of a free market economy, where producers are free to make whatever they can sell and in which buyers can buy whatever they want and can afford. They support a mixed economy of state and privately owned industry and services.

Both of these views emphasise the importance of citizenship and the individual's participation in society. Both endorse policies that promote social inclusion through the eradication of the five giants of evil (want, disease, squalor, ignorance and idleness) identified by Beveridge in 1942.

The Liberal Democrats Party

This was formed from an alliance between the old Liberal Party and those members of both the Labour and Conservative parties whose beliefs and values tended towards a middle ground. Its policies reflect elements of both parties (which makes coalition possible), but its position on education is broadly a liberal and egalitarian one.

The Conservative Party

The Conservative Party is similar to the Labour Party in that it acts as an umbrella for various different factions. Again, for the sake of clarity, these groups have been placed under two main headings, the neoliberal and the neoconservative tendencies.

Neoliberal beliefs

To the right of the centre point on the main continuum the neoliberal element believes in the freedom of choice for consumers within a free market economy. In a free market, competition is seen as a good thing as it ensures that goods and services are produced as efficiently as possible so that prices find their 'correct' (lowest) level. The market is seen as something that will regulate itself; demand will stimulate production and lack of demand will result in less production. The state should, therefore, interfere in the economy as little as possible. The neoliberals also believe that individuals have free will and can 'help themselves' to achieve their aims in life. For them the role of the state is to facilitate equality of opportunity rather than to ensure equality of outcomes for individuals. For example, the state will provide education but it is up to the individual to make the best use of it.

Neoconservative beliefs

To the right of the neoliberals are the neoconservatives whose ideology is more difficult to define. In general it is opposed to central government intervention (big government) in the economy but it also accepts the importance of a limited number of social welfare objectives. Neoconservatives emphasise the importance of individual efforts to achieve and get on in society and believe that the role of the state is simply to provide a safety net of support for those who are unable to provide for themselves.

The major influences affecting politics and policy

In all of these views you can see that the relationship between the economy and the state is central; but other factors can have a tremendous influence on politics and policy. Changes in technology (the introduction of computers), scientific advances (new medicines and cures) and social changes (the greater role of women in society) also need to be taken into account when considering how politics and policy shape education and inclusion in education. For simplicity, the next section uses a historical framework to help you make your own judgements about the response of FE to inclusion in five main periods: post-war reconstruction; the inter-party period; the Conservative administration; New Labour and the current Coalition.

Post-war reconstruction (1945–mid-1950s)

Critical thinking activity: the role of education in post-war Britain

» *Thinking about the period immediately after the Second World War, what challenges do you think the education system must have faced?*

You may know that the Second World War left Britain with a legacy of a ruined economy and a society that was in need of change. The political parties all agreed that change was necessary in order to build a better society which improved the rights and living conditions of the individual. Their commitment to a new society became clear in the pioneering legislation of the welfare state under which benefits to society such as healthcare and housing were to be funded through taxation and delivered free to those in need. A separate piece of legislation, but one which saw education as a social benefit, was introduced in 1944 and became known as Butler's Education Act. This Act formed the foundation for the compulsory education system in England and much of the UK for the rest of the twentieth century. It was based on the idea of equality of access to opportunity by providing education for all at both primary and secondary levels. However, in addition to providing general education the system was also expected to shoulder wider social responsibilities for the welfare of students. Legislation meant that schools had a role in monitoring and supporting the health and well-being of students through the introduction of a system of free medical and dental inspections and the provision of free milk and subsidised (or free for those eligible) hot midday meals. Clothing grants for uniforms and subsidised transport for students also became part of the wider social remit for the education system.

Butler saw education as a tool for social improvement and a way of promoting equality of opportunity. In his vision FE had a central role as a provider of pathways to self-improvement for those who had completed their compulsory education. Two clear pathways or directions for FE were introduced: vocational education and community education. The vocational pathway was linked to the need to rebuild the economy by introducing education on a part-time basis for those between 15 and 18 who were not participating in some form of education (such as an apprenticeship). This pathway was underpinned by the belief that a more skilled workforce would contribute directly or indirectly to economic growth. The second pathway for FE was that of community-based education. Local Education Authorities (LEAs) were tasked with providing subsidised *leisure time occupation in ... organised cultural training and rec-reative activities ... for any person over compulsory school age ... able and willing to profit by the facilities provided for that purpose* (Trowler, 1998, p 20).

Critical thinking activity: inclusion and the new education system

»   *Thinking about what you have just read, what do you think the post-war role of FE was in relation to inclusion?*

A more inclusive system?

You may have concluded that, in addition to improving the economy, FE had a significant role in promoting social inclusion by offering personal development opportunities to everyone – including the majority of women and working-class men – who would not traditionally have considered any form of post-compulsory education. However, you could also argue that in many respects the new system disguised rather than challenged existing inequalities. The 1944 Act also introduced what became known as the tripartite system of education. At the age of 11, children took the eleven-plus exam, a form of 'intelligence test' which meant that they were sent to different types of schools (grammar, secondary or technical) depending on their type of intelligence (academic, technical or practical). This division was intended to ensure that all children went into the type of secondary education that was best suited to their abilities. You may feel that this was an unfair system. As Tomlinson (2001) points out, it not only met the economic needs of the times but also both mirrored and reinforced the prevailing class structure. The changes in the compulsory education system, together with a larger HE provision designed to cater for the academically able, meant that FE became a sector whose primary function was to provide technical and vocational skills to students whose future employment, as Wilkinson (1945, in Jones, 2003, p 24) the then Minister of Education noted, would not *demand any measure of technical skill or knowledge.*

The inter-party period (mid-1950s–1979)

The inter-party period was a time of considerable political uncertainty which saw three Labour and three Conservative administrations over a period of approximately 25 years. In general, the late 1950s and early 1960s were periods of optimism and change in compulsory educa-tion, with the growth of liberal and progressive methods of student-centred and mixed-ability instruction in schools. A new type of school, the Comprehensive, was also introduced which combined grammar and secondary modern schools into one school catering for all children in a geographical area. New qualifications (the Certificate in Secondary Education) which contained an element of course work were also introduced as an alternative to the existing exam-based GCE system.

The position of Further Education

The FE provision of this period was largely community based with colleges co-operating closely with local firms and communities. In the booming economy of the early part of this period FE catered mainly for those in employment taking craft qualifications on a part-time basis. Those teaching in FE had considerable discretion in developing courses that reflected the needs of the local area, and in using the methods that they felt most appropriate in teaching these courses. The period was one of immense social change, with growing numbers of women entering the labour market and increasing levels of immigration from newly independent Commonwealth countries. FE colleges were encouraged to respond to this social upheaval by broadening their curriculum and increasing the range of vocational qualifications as well as offering academic subjects. This allowed colleges to include a rising number of young, full-time students, and an increasing proportion of female and black minority ethnic (BME) students, and to challenge the underlying social stereotypes of gender, race and class by promoting inclusion.

You will remember from the last section that the post-war government was committed to providing better housing and welfare for all members of society. Massive government spending to meet these commitments initially led to a huge demand for labour, but during the 1960s this stimulus began to fade. At the same time the traditional manufacturing base of the UK economy was being challenged by foreign competition and the rapid development of new technologies. These changes were accompanied by a gradual realisation that the UK had to compete more effectively in a global economy and that the type of labour needed to do this was skilled rather than unskilled. Unemployment began to rise (particularly youth unemployment, which jumped from 10,000 in 1974 to 240,000 in 1977) as a result of the changing demands of the economy. The taxes the government gathered from those in work were no longer sufficient to sustain government expenditure on welfare state provisions such as unemployment benefits and education.

The demand for a repositioning of Further Education

As the economy rapidly declined, the demand for traditional day-release schemes fell too, and FE became widely criticised by those who felt that the skills and training it supplied no longer matched the requirements of the economy. This was summarised in a vitriolic attack on FE by Harold Wilson (leader of the ruling Labour Party, 1964–70) in a speech now generally referred to as the 'white heat of technology' speech in 1963. In this speech he criticised FE for its confusion and proliferation of courses, its high part-time attendance and low retention rates. FE was widely seen to be ineffective in supporting growth and innovation in the economy; as the economy continued to weaken there were increasing demands for FE standards to be raised by increasing the accountability, efficiency and effectiveness of the sector. Having read this you may feel that it all sounds horribly familiar and I'm sure you will be able to draw many parallels between what was happening in this period and what is happening in FE now.

The changing role of education as a tool for inclusion

Before moving on, it is important that you also note that during this period several landmark pieces of legislation guaranteeing the rights of the individual and promoting social inclusion were passed, such as the Equal Pay Act 1970, the Sex Discrimination Act 1975 and the Race Relations Act 1976. All of these Acts had an impact on FE, but possibly the greatest influence on inclusion during this period resulted from a Report rather than an Act of Parliament. The Warnock Report, which dealt with the education of students with special educational needs (SEN), was published during the last gasp of the Labour administration in May 1978. The Report was an attempt to guarantee equality of treatment and opportunity for disabled children by integrating them into state schools wherever possible. The Report was a significant one for education at all levels. The notion of 'statementing' was introduced in order to determine additional support needs for individual students. This resulted in a massive rise in the number of students recognised as needing support and consequently in huge demand for LSA provision. The Report was also eventually responsible for the closure of many specialist schools, bringing a new type of student into mainstream education with special educational needs that teachers had not necessarily been trained to work with. This Report defined both the concept and direction of inclusion within the education system and potentially led to other, more structural elements of possible exclusion, such as gender and racial equality, becoming embedded as areas for challenge within education.

Critical thinking activity: the impact of ideology

Consider what you have just learnt about the way that government policy affected FE in terms of inclusive practice in the post-war and inter-party period.

»   *What seemed to be the major factors influencing educational policy in the last part of the inter-party period?*

The Conservative administration (1979–97)

The 'business' of education

Following the 'winter of discontent' (1978–79), the Conservative Party led by Thatcher swept to power with a large majority. This signalled the start of a new phase in the development of FE. The Conservative administration was initially neoliberal in its outlook and, as you will remember, this meant that it had a strong commitment to a free market economy, public accountability, economy and efficiency. These are not easy concepts, but if you think of them as competition and consumer choice, value for money and added value you will see how they came to influence education policy. FE had been publicly criticised by all the political parties for its inefficiency, waste and irrelevant and outdated provision, and it was a prime target for modernisation. FE was initially removed from the remit of LEAs and put under the control of a government agency – the Manpower Services Commission (MSC) – which assumed responsibility for the funding of vocational education and training, employment and enterprise. Although this was technically an independent organisation, it allowed the government to shape the sector without appearing directly responsible for MSC decision-making.

Vocationalism

You are probably familiar with National Vocational Qualifications (NVQs) and you may even teach on these types of courses which were introduced during this period. For the first time, employers were directly involved in shaping education in FE. The competence statements of these qualifications were devised in conjunction with employers to ensure that they matched the requirements of the workplace, and they were funded by the government. Government investment in training was designed to yield dividends in the future through the development of a mobile, flexible and skilled workforce. Vocational skills became seen as collections of separate and often generic competences. Once an individual had learned the skills and been accredited as competent they could carry them with them as they moved from one employer to another. However, Lea (2003) suggests that the introduction of NVQs had other consequences. He suggests that they resulted in an increasing separation between academic and vocational education and in the lowering of expectation and prospects for those following the vocational training route.

As you have seen, by changing the funding mechanisms to support the NVQ system the government gained control of a large part of the FE curriculum and firmly aligned its future to that of the economy. You could also argue that by introducing NVQs the government had introduced a system of training in FE that was no longer designed to challenge, but rather to reinforce, existing social and economic inequality.

Competition

You will remember that between 1979 and 1997 government was committed to competition and consumer choice. In an effort to reduce youth unemployment the government also made it possible to gain NVQs through private training agencies and this introduced both choice and competition into the FE sector. This strand of policy was developed with the introduction of the Further and Higher Education Act 1992 under which FE became a supplier of learning with students as 'consumers' of educational products (qualifications). FE colleges became private businesses competing for customers in an educational 'market' that also consisted of sixth forms, training providers and suppliers of community education such as the LEA. Funding was restricted and provided only for what became known as Schedule 2 courses; that is, those which were vocational or work related and which led to recognised qualifications. As we saw above, the government was committed to two other things: value for money and added value. By changing funding for FE so that colleges had to concentrate on ensuring students achieved specific qualifications, the government aimed to make sure the sector was giving value for money; and by introducing competition it prompted FE to introduce added value to its courses in order to attract students.

Public accountability

The reforms in funding and the introduction of new qualifications meant that effectively the government controlled the curriculum in FE. Although political rhetoric suggested that the aim was to increase competition and consumer choice, Randall (1992) argues that in reality the colleges' level of freedom was similar to that *which business people gain through franchising from a Pizza Hut multi-national*. As you saw above, one of the government's aims was to increase public accountability. The government's control over qualifications and funding gave them enough information to introduce a system of league tables. These measured levels of achievement in the sector and allowed both the government and the public to compare providers. In addition, an inspection system was introduced to monitor the quality of the provision. This new inspection process meant that the government could both *define* and *measure* what was meant by quality in FE and also monitor it through the publication of inspection reports.

This combination of government initiatives to meet government commitments had the effect of redefining the public's perception of FE. It was now operating in a competitive environment as it contended for students with schools and employers and it had been made publicly accountable through the inspection process. The funding mechanisms had forced it to become more efficient and concentrate on economically viable courses. Rather than being perceived as an aid to building an inclusive society it was now regarded by the government as an economic asset.

Critical thinking activity: the impact of Conservatism on Further Education

» *What impact do you think these reforms may have had on inclusion within the FE sector?*

The New Labour era

When you were thinking about this question you may have come to the conclusion that the purpose of FE, which had been clearly defined in the post-war era, had changed significantly with the major emphasis now being on meeting economic needs rather than on promoting social inclusion. However, the political climate changed with the fall of the Conservative administration and the introduction of a government with a new political philosophy, and once again the role of FE was redefined.

The 'Third Way'

After a long period in the political wilderness the Labour Party was elected to power in 1997 under the banner of 'Third Way' politics. The 'Third Way' was a path between state control of the economy as advocated by the socialists and the fully free market economy of the neo-liberal conservatives. The 'Third Way' aimed at a competitive and efficient market-based economy combined with a social justice agenda that emphasised the rights and responsibilities of the individual. In a competitive economy the state would continue to provide welfare services such as education and health, which would then support individuals to play their part in the development of a fair and just civil society.

'Education, Education, Education'

Entering into power with the mantra of 'Education, Education, Education' the Blair government claimed commitment to placing education at the heart of the political agenda and to giving *everyone the chance through education, training and work, to realise their full potential, and thus build an inclusive and fair society and a competitive economy* (DfEE, 1998). Some of you will remember the rapid changes in education policy at the time: the development of nursery education, Sure Start schemes, curriculum changes, new qualifications, new forms of specialist schools and academies, and an increase in the number expected to attend university. All of these reforms were intended to extend inclusion of the socially disadvantaged.

The social justice agenda

A series of reports by luminaries such as Tomlinson (1996), Kennedy (1997), Fryer (1997), Dearing (1994) and Moser (1998) identified areas of economic and social weakness at a national level. Three major initiatives were designed to have a major impact on the provision of post-16 education and training. Skills for Life (2001) introduced strategies for improving adult literacy and numeracy; Success for All (2002) focused on improving the post-16 education and training provision; and 21st Century Skills (2003) examined ways of closing the skills gap between the UK and its competitors in the global market.

Widening participation

To meet the government's new economic and social aims FE was required to increase access to education by widening participation. The objective of widening participation was to provide accessible education for those who had been *subject to the selective and alienating processes of formal education* (Tomlinson, 2001, p 114), or who were excluded from the labour market due to their lack of basic/employability skills, learning or physical differences. To ensure that teachers in FE were able to work effectively with previously marginalised groups, measures to modernise and professionalise the workforce were also introduced.

Critical thinking activity: policy points

» *Have a look on the internet for some summaries of one or two of the Reports or Acts mentioned above and list their major points.*

» *Think about the implications of these points for FE in terms of inclusion, the students and the staff.*

New plans and old foundations

The intention of these reforms, many of which may have affected you as a student or a teacher, was undoubtedly to promote social inclusion through education. If you think back to the post-war government you will see that they share many of the objectives of that time. FE was once again seen as an engine for social inclusion, but there were some significant differences between the 'Third Way' and the post-war aims. Although the government was committed to social and personal inclusion through education, it continued with many of the measures initiated by the Conservatives. The ideas of a competitive market and individual choice were retained, and the inspection regime was strengthened so that it could set targets and monitor change in FE colleges as well as measure value for money. Initially, with a strong economy and a full treasury, the government was able to fund measures for social justice. However, as the economy began to slow down, the demands made on FE to promote social inclusion again began to conflict with the demands for improvements in its efficiency, effectiveness and accountability.

Increasingly the learning 'delivered' in the sector became driven by a *culture of credentialisation* (Lumby and Wilson, 2003, p 539) where the colleges' success was seen in terms of the number of qualifications achieved by students. FE came under continued pressure to move away from the culture of meeting the needs and requirements of students unless they could be met through achieving a qualification of some sort. Colleges within the sector continued to operate as independent businesses, however, strategies such as the Skills for Life initiative (2001) placed pressure on the sector to ensure that centrally designed materials and teaching practices were used to develop national standards of delivery.

The increased role of Further Education in facilitating social inclusion

Although FE began to be criticised again by employers for not meeting the needs of the economy, in the first years of this century the government continued to develop its role in social inclusion. Following the Foster Report (2004) FE was given additional responsibilities to tackle low post-16 participation in education by re-engaging disaffected students. This initiative, as you may well remember, was supported by the introduction of the Educational Maintenance Allowance (EMA) in 2004 to help students pay for travel, etc.; and by a refocusing of the qualifications to ensure that functional skills were included. By making these changes colleges were intended to realise ... [their] ... potential to be a key driver of economic growth and competitiveness and an engine of social justice and equality of opportunity (DfES, 2006, p 13). If you teach basic or functional skills you may also remember another policy that affected FE at this time: the changes to the New Deal and Train to Gain initiatives for adult students. Under these changes free tuition was made available to some categories of adults who needed basic education skills to attain work. In the government's view FE was central to the skills, employability and social justice agendas. However, at this point you might also like to consider an alternative view – that rather than being a driving force for inclusion, FE had simply become a means of patching up students who had been failed by the compulsory education system.

Legislation for inclusion

Although the sector was predominantly seen as a means of providing training in skills and basic education, it was also influenced by the wider demands of New Labour's social inclusion policies. Following the publication of the Macpherson Report (1999) into institutional racism after the death of Stephen Lawrence, colleges were required to produce anti-racism policies. The death of Victoria Climbié and the subsequent Laming Inquiry (2003) led to colleges reviewing their safeguarding procedures and working more closely with other welfare services. More specifically, the Special Educational Needs and Disability Act 2001 compelled colleges to review their policies to ensure that students with disabilities were not disadvantaged in relation to the education and other services that the colleges provided. In line with the government need for transparency, all of these became areas for scrutiny under the inspection regime then in operation.

Critical thinking activity

» List some of the tensions that you feel existed for colleges as a result of them being inclusive and being a business.

» What impact do you think these tensions may have had on colleges' attitudes towards inclusion?

» What impact do you feel that the changes may have had on the role of staff in FE?

The Coalition

The three New Labour governments all placed considerable emphasis on the role of education in promoting social inclusion and directed resources towards reforming the various sectors, particularly FE. However, although FE's role in social inclusion was maintained and even extended, its ability to effect social change had been damaged by its need to compete in the post-16 education market in order to survive. As you saw in the inter-party period, a downturn in the economy meant that spending on welfare services in general and on education in particular had to be reduced, and this pattern was repeated under the Coalition government.

The Coalition government is influenced by neoliberal beliefs of consumer choice and a free market. This has led to changes in compulsory education and the new Academy and Free School systems have introduced a new element of competition and choice. Although FE now has to compete with these new institutions for post-16 students, you may feel that the Coalition view of the role for FE is quite traditional. For the Coalition, FE's primary purpose appears to be to equip *people with the basic, applied and specialist skills they need in the world of work, either at the beginning of their careers, or when they need re-skilling* (Cabinet Office, 2013, p 17). However, rather than training apprentices predominantly within FE, under the Skills for Sustainable Growth (2010) initiative, the emphasis is now on the development of employment-based apprenticeships at level 3. In an echo of the measures taken under the Thatcher administrations, the Wolf Report (2011) recommended a rationalisation of the qualification system to reduce the number of courses and focus them on the needs of employers in terms of standards and content. Again, this has been supported by a change in the funding regime which currently attaches funding to the student rather than concentrating on funding outputs by qualification, so now FE must compete effectively in the post-16 education market to attract students.

Other financial reforms have had a significant impact on the sector's ability to influence inclusion. Younger students are no longer entitled to the EMA payments as a right (although your students who are experiencing hardship may be able to access some funding through the college's discretionary funding pot). There continues to be a minimal provision for funding for specific categories of students with functional skills needs, but the majority of our older students now have to take responsibility for funding their own education through a loans system. The impact of these reforms on the inclusive ethos of the sector has been considerable with reduced numbers of students (both young and more mature) entering education and training. It might appear that once again the pendulum for FE has swung away from its role in inclusion to one of servicing the economy.

Conclusion

Since the introduction of the welfare state, the role of FE in relation to inclusion has been varied. At times FE has taken centre stage in the struggle to create an inclusive society, and at other times it has been relegated to the chorus. Although seen by many people as the 'second chance sector' for disadvantaged students, FE has struggled to maintain this ethos and to maintain its 'open doors' policy, wholeheartedly welcoming all and any who wish to pursue vocational, recreational or academic courses. Consistently positioned and repositioned in relation to the economy, it has been transformed from a social service to a business existing in the virtual reality of the marketplace for education. But FE still remains dependent upon and largely controlled by the government through funding. Somehow, in the midst of all this change and uncertainty, the majority of staff in FE remain committed to a culture of inclusion and the right of all to be able to access education and training. While that remains the case, the sector will continue to have an important role in building a more inclusive society.

Chapter reflections

»   *The influence of the political context on the sector is immense and inconsistent.*

»   *The role of FE in relation to inclusion has varied according to the prevailing political climate.*

»   *FE has at times been (and continues to be) a tool used by government to promote inclusion in society.*

»   *There is often tension between the ethos of inclusion in the sector and the economic imperatives that policy defines.*

Taking it further

Ball, S (2010) New Class Inequalities in Education: Why Education Policy may be Looking in the Wrong Place! Education Policy, Civil Society and Social Class. *International Journal of Sociology and Social Policy*, 30(3/4): 155–66.

An interesting, instructive and informative text detailing educational policy until the end of the twentieth century.

Trowler, P (1998) *Education Policy: A Policy Sociology Approach*. Eastbourne: Gildredge Press Ltd.

Not an easy read but an insightful analysis of recent policy and its impact on society.

References

Ball, J (2013) *Education, Justice and Democracy: The Struggle Over Ignorance and Opportunity*. London: Centre for Labour and Social Studies.

Ball, S (1990) *Politics and Policy Making in Education*. London: Routledge.

Ball, S (2003) The Teacher's Soul and the Terrors of Performativity. *Journal of Education Policy*, 18(2): 215–28.

Ball, S (2010) New Class Inequalities in Education: Why Education Policy may be Looking in the Wrong Place! Education Policy, Civil Society and Social Class. *International Journal of Sociology and Social Policy*, 30(3/4): 155–66.

Bartlett, S and Burton, D (2012) *Introduction to Education Studies*. London: Sage.

Dearing, R (1994) *The National Curriculum and its Assessment: Final Report*. London: School Curriculum and Assessment Authority.

DfEE (1998) *Select Committee on Environmental Audit Third Report*. Available at www.publications. parliament.uk/pa/cm199899/cmselect/cmenvaud/92/92app04.htm

DfES (2006) *Further Education: Raising Skills, Improving Life Chances*. London: The Stationery Office.

Freire, P (1966) *Pedagogy of the Oppressed*. London: Penguin Books.

Fryer, R H (1997) *Learning for the Twenty-First Century*. London: NAGCELL.

Jones, K (2003) *Education in Britain: 1944 to the Present*. Cambridge: Polity Press.

Kennedy, H (1997) *Learning Works: Widening Participation in Further Education*. Coventry: FEFC.

Lea, J (2003) Overview: Post compulsory Education in Context in Lea, J et al. (2003) *Working in Post Compulsory Education*. Maidenhead: Open University Press.

Lumby, J and Wilson, M (2003) Developing 14–19 Education: Meeting Needs and Improving Choices. *Journal of Education Policy*, 18(5): 533–50.

Moser, C (1999) *A Fresh Start: Improving Literacy and Numeracy*. London: Department for Education and Employment.

Randall, C (1992) *Training and Enterprise Councils – An Exercise in Illusion, Exclusion and Class Elision*. Centre for a Working World Discussion Paper 6, Sheffield: The Centre for a Working World.

Sharpe, T (1978) *Wilt*. London: Pan Books Ltd.

Tomlinson, J (1996) *Inclusive Learning: Report of the Learning Difficulties and/or Disabilities Committee*. London: HMSO.

Tomlinson, S (2001) *Education in the Post-Welfare Society*. Buckingham: Open University Press.

Trowler, P (1998) *Education Policy: A Policy Sociology Approach*. Eastbourne: Gildredge Press Ltd.

Wolf, A (2011) *Review of Vocational Education: The Wolf Report*. London: The Stationery Office.

Websites

Cabinet Office (2013) *Mid-term Review*. Available at http://midtermreview.cabinetoffice.gov.uk/fixing-the-economy/universities-and-further-education/index.html.

4 New teachers – old ideas?

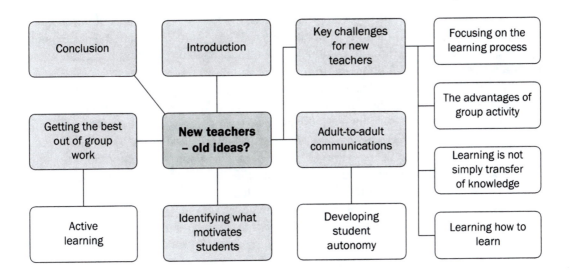

Chapter aims

Most of the teachers who come into FE are mature people. Many of them have been successful in their previous career and feel they have a great deal of skills and knowledge that they would like to pass on to the next generation. However, being a teacher in FE is not just about knowing your subject, and many new entrants to the profession are bewildered by the number of roles they are expected to fulfil and genuinely surprised at the range of their duties. The purpose of this chapter is to encourage you to think about the challenges that these teachers face in implementing inclusive practices, to help you to reflect on the influence that the teacher has on learning (and students!) and to look at social learning as a means of helping students to learn.

Introduction

Well, some days I feel as though I work at confused dot com – in some sort of parallel universe. It isn't a bit what I thought it would be like, that's for sure. That was the response to my *How's it going?* question at the beginning of a tutorial. One of the great things about my job as a student-educator is that I get the chance to talk to new teachers; to discover not only what they feel they are learning but also where they are 'coming from' in terms of their expectations of themselves, the students and the work that they do. In tutorials I learn about their emotional highs and lows, their challenges and their successes, what's going well and what's driving them crazy. Sometimes tutorials are a chance to celebrate with them when they feel that they have achieved something personally, but more often than not they want to talk about the vicarious pleasure they get from seeing their students succeed. At other times it's an opportunity for them to just talk, for me to listen and commiserate with them, or just let them offload, to let them tell someone *who gives a damn* (my student's words – not mine!) about what is happening to them and how they feel. Frequently in the early stages of their course and careers they use the first few minutes of tutorials to vent their feelings, express concerns or to seek reassurance or guidance; but there are repeated similarities in the anxieties new teachers express. Teaching techniques and classroom management are generally high on the agenda in these early meetings, but in almost all instances new teachers express a mounting concern that the students they are working with are not responding to their input in the way that they anticipated and they are struggling to find ways to 'connect' with students. They feel students need more from them to help them to learn.

CASE STUDY

The painting and decorating lecturer's tale – working in the classroom

The lecturer's view

Mick worked for many years as a self-employed decorator, but due to a change in his personal circumstances a couple of years ago he took a job as an instructor in a prison working with adults who were following NVQ programmes as part of their sentence planning regime. He got *bitten by the teaching bug*, as he described it, when he was interviewed for the Diploma in Teaching and the Lifelong Learning Sector (DTLLS) course. He is now a vocational lecturer and has been working in the Painting and Decorating (P&D) area of the Construction department at an FE college for three months. He works with students aged between 16 and 18 who are following a vocational course at levels 1, 2 and 3 in painting and decorating, and while he is happy teaching the practical skills, he admits that he finds the theory-based sessions in the classroom challenging. Unfortunately his colleague in the P&D department is away sick and Mick is now coping with all of the groups with only a part-time lecturer to assist him. He had been preparing the students for the phase tests conducted at the end of each unit and had completed a mock assessment with the level 1 group before he came for his tutorial. He was feeling very frustrated by the whole experience.

I can't understand it! I just don't understand. Why aren't they learning? I teach them all the right theory and they should know it but they don't. Every time I give them a test they get the answers wrong, because they just don't listen. I've told them over and over again. So why aren't they learning? It was worse than ever this morning, they knew they'd got a test and I'd told them exactly what to revise but what happened? Half of them didn't turn up and three of them just gave up after five minutes and said they couldn't do any more because it was too difficult. It took me all afternoon the other day going round to different people in the college to find out what I had to do to get these mock phase tests set up. They are multiple-choice tests and they have to be done on a computer just like the real thing so I had to book the right rooms, fill in all the requests for people to support the ones that struggle with reading to make it real for them, and then get someone to set up all the machines for me. I don't know why I bother sometimes – I really don't. I came here to make a difference; I honestly thought I could give something back and that the kids I would be teaching would really want to learn, just like I did, but I just don't seem to be able to get through to them. What do they want me to do? I feel as though I'm spoon-feeding them already. They just don't seem to be interested – what am I doing wrong?

The observer's view

Following his tutorial Mick agreed with his tutor that an additional, supportive, non-judgemental observation of his teaching would be useful in helping him to identify problem areas and work out ways of improving his classroom practice. The tutor suggested that it would be useful for him to be observed working with the same group in both theory and practical lessons. During the theory lesson the following points were raised for discussion by the observing tutor.

- The desks are in rows – limits the opportunity for interaction. Computers (limited number) are around the wall on two sides of the classroom.

- Only ten students in – one came in late (not challenged) – four absent for no reason.

- Students are expected to take notes throughout the session.

- The lecturer is talking at them not to them! No two-way communication.

- Presentation and demonstration are didactic – chalk and talk.

- The students are bored – two have mobile phones out under the desk and learners texting.

- Little interaction between the learners and the lecturer.

- Handouts long and closely typed.

- No group activities.

- Workbook is followed without question. Only assessment of learning is the workbook. No differentiation – no extension activities.

- Theory lesson – no connections made between the theory and workshop/real-world application.

- English and mathematics left to the Learning Support Assistants (LSAs) to explain – LSAs doing most of the work for some students!

- Interactive white board – but no use is made of it other than to show a presentation.

Critical thinking activity: identifying the challenges

» *Having read through the case study, what do you feel are the key challenges that Mick faces in his new role?*

Key challenges for new teachers

When you were reading the case study you might have felt that you had encountered a lot of the problems that Mick was facing. Generally speaking, most of the problems that all new teachers face can be put into the two categories which Young and Lucas (in Mortimore, 1999) identify as:

1. those that are narrowly focused on inclusive practices in the classroom; and

2. those that are focused on more general issues of professionalism.

In the inclusive practices category there are two main concerns. The first of these is the transition that many teachers (and this may include you) have to make from being transmitters of teaching to becoming managers of the learning process – the move from teacher-centred to student-centred methods of teaching. The second, and for many the more challenging, is the need for them to include core subjects like English and mathematics in their teaching. Many new teachers don't expect this; after all, they came into FE to teach their own specialism, not English, mathematics, employability skills, etc. The more general challenges about professionalism can also be worrying for new teachers. Coming into FE a new teacher has to make the move from an intra-professional view of professionalism to an inter-professional view. They have to move from working as a professional in their own vocational area to a situation where they are expected to support and be supported by professionals who are experts in linked but separate areas. For example, to support their students the new teacher may have to forge links with IT technicians within the college and with external partners such as local employers who may be in a position to offer work placement opportunities to their students. For some new teachers this partnership is quite unexpected, but it does help them to gain connective knowledge which is useful to their students as they are able to show how the subject that they are teaching fits into wider society.

In talking about the problems he has encountered in his teaching, and from the discussion points made by the observing tutor, it would seem that Mick has unwittingly faced several of these challenges. However, at this stage of his career Mick's main concern, and that of his tutor, is centred around the students and the difficulty he feels he is having in including them in the learning process, something which is evidenced in his final *cri de coeur* – *They don't seem to be interested – what am I doing wrong?*

Focusing on the learning process

You will have noticed in Mick's comments that he is giving his students the same information *over and over* again, and from this you may surmise that he is concentrating on the teaching rather than the learning process in the classroom. All of us have to cope with the requirement to get our students through their qualifications, but for a new teacher, as you may have found when you first came into FE, this pressure is very difficult to cope with. In an effort to *get through the content ... against a strict and unforgiving assessment deadline* (Butcher, 2005, p 108) Mick has become a director rather than a manager of learning, an attitude that can rule out the potential for students to be included in the learning process.

Most of our students have made the move into FE at a point of disjunction in their life; they may have recognised the need to obtain new skills in order to progress, or they may want a change of direction. In Mick's case his students are making the transition from school to work and are entering into a new chapter in their learning career. Mick's students may feel empowered by moving into FE, but they are moving from the safety of familiar social and cultural environments to an environment that may for some bring back negative memories of their previous experience of education. In the initial stages of a course of study the majority of students in FE colleges are putting themselves at a substantial level of psychological risk and they are very aware of their vulnerability in their position as a new student. In this new, and for some, potentially threatening setting, gaining subject knowledge alone is not enough and they need to develop other skills and wider forms of learning to enable them to climb Maslow's Hierarchy of Needs (1954) and achieve self-actualisation through academic success.

The advantages of group activity

Learning itself is an individual and generally self-directed process that happens when individuals succeed in 'making meaning' (developing their own understanding) of new knowledge or skills. We all want our students to develop from what Knowles (1980) describes as the state of the dependent-self (dependent for learning on the teacher) to that of being self-directed students who take control of, and accept responsibility for, their learning. This requires a good deal of self-confidence (something that you may find is lacking in many of the students you work with) and it can be helpful if they work with others so that they are able to discuss their understanding of new things and check that they are on the right track. Social learning, for the purposes of this chapter, is defined as any and all learning that takes place in group situations. Social learning acknowledges the importance of social contact and informal learning in gaining understanding or making meaning. In this student-centred process there are two key components: contact with others and the exploration of the self.

Learning is not simply transfer of knowledge

For social learning to take place Young and Lucas (1999) argue that four major conditions must be met.

1. The knowledge to be acquired must be *new*, not merely a reflection of past learning.

2. The acquisition of learning must be a *process*, not simply the transfer of knowledge.

3. Learning should take place *with others*, to facilitate discussion and meaning making.

4. Students must have access to concepts and ideas that enable them to form a *framework* for the learning.

If you re-read the case study and apply these conditions to Mick's current practice you'll see that, although most of the learning that he provides in painting and decorating will be new to his students, the other conditions are only being partially fulfilled. His current pedagogic practice is based largely on the 'empty vessels' idea noted by Freire (1972) in his banking model of learning where students are seen as empty containers which the teacher has to fill with knowledge, a model that reinforces the dependency of the student on the teacher.

Critical thinking activity: involving the student in learning

»   *Make notes about how you feel Mick can embed the other conditions of learning noted above in his practice.*

»   *How can he include his students?*

»   *How can he develop self-directed rather than dependent students?*

In your notes you may well have mentioned the need for Mick to include the students in the learning process. Your suggestions for doing this may have included such things as group work, student-focused activities, making theory 'real' by connecting it with practice or wider objectives, differentiation, etc. For learning to take place it needs to have some personal significance for the student. In the case of Mick's students, they have all made a conscious decision to follow the course, probably to gain employment in the long run, and so the learning is important to them. Theory or underpinning knowledge, as most teachers will agree, once it is mastered, provides students with a series of generic tools that they can use in different situations. It is *transferable*. However, as the observing tutor has noted, in isolation theory lessons can be boring for students. As Kolb's Learning Cycle (1984) suggests, to assimilate and understand new knowledge students not only have to think about it but they also need to put their new learning into practice. Regrettably, however, in most FE colleges 'theory' and 'practical' sessions are separated on the timetable (and consequently in the minds of students) and one of the most difficult tasks facing teachers is to bridge this divide to not only facilitate students' understanding of theory but to enable them to relate it to practice.

Learning how to learn

You will have noted from the case study that most of the students Mick works with are young adults in the process of making the difficult transition into adulthood. Like many of the students that you work with, they are beginning to encounter 'adult' problems such as money and time management, but they are gradually developing the skills and strategies to solve them. Although these skills can be used by the clever teacher (this is you!) to embed learning by setting subject-related problems for students, there may be a need for students to 'learn how to learn'. Students need to understand how they learn and develop their thinking skills. One way that you might help them to do this is to encourage them to reflect on what they are doing so that they correct themselves. Bartlett and Burton (2012, p 232) describe this as students developing *a commentator in the[ir] … mind who analyses and comments upon the methods they are using to learn a new concept or skill while the learning is happening.*

Bruner (1996) suggests that if challenging concepts are presented in a way that they understand, your students will grasp them, especially if you support them by scaffolding their journey, explaining the process step by step. When you act as a guide it helps students to develop a framework for the new learning. By helping them to reflect on and assess the information you enable them to make the learning meaningful. This scaffolding process will act as a model for development of their own 'commentator' while helping them to understand. One framework that might be used in this context is that of the six thinking hats process suggested by de Bono (1985) which helps the development of structured thinking in group situations. Each hat denotes a different stage in the process of problem solving (the collection of facts, the use of intuition, critical analysis, logical development, creative thinking and decision-making). By using the hats (or even wearing them if you have enough) students become part of the learning process. By working through a process of 'messy thinking' with other students they are able to access theory and also apply it to a vocationally related problem.

The Pygmalion effect

All teachers have expectations of their students. The 'Pygmalion effect' (Rosenthal and Jacobson, 1968) of teachers' expectations on students and learning is widely recognised. If teachers expect a great deal of a student that student generally achieves higher results than others of whom the teacher has lower expectations. If you think about your own practice you may find that this pattern exists with your students. When you read the case study you will have noticed that Mick started his career in FE with the expectation that his students would be as keen to learn as he himself had been as a student. His comment that he feels that he is *spoon-feeding them already* seems to indicate that his expectations of his students have been dramatically lowered. His obvious frustration with this situation, together with his self-imposed role as a director rather than a manager of learning, is neither conducive to him including his students in the learning process nor to helping them to become the self-directed students he expects them to be. Although it may not be obvious to either Mick or his students, his frustrations appear to have led him to act in what Berne (1961) describes as the *parent* in his transactions with his students, placing them in the role of *children* to be taught rather than to learn.

Adult-to-adult communications

Berne's theory of transactional analysis is a theory of communication that looks at patterns of communication or transactions between people. According to Berne there are three ego states (patterns of behaviour and thinking that influence communication) which exist in all individuals. Each state – the parent, the adult and the child – represents a pattern of communication that has a particular function and uses a specific type of language. The parental ego state uses the language of values, the adult uses the language of logic and rationality and the child uses that of emotion. Each transaction, or communication, between individuals is initiated by a stimulus which generates a response. If the response is complementary, that is, if the sender of the message receives the response from the anticipated ego state, then the transaction is successful. For example, if the teacher is communicating with students from the point of view of an adult and receives an adult response from the students, then the transaction is successful. However, if the teacher receives a childish response from the students who seem to be angry, petulant or defiant, then communication between them has not been successful and the transaction can be described as being crossed. A teacher adopting a parental tone (for example, scolding or over-directive) is likely to trigger a childish response (for example, rebellious, sulky or helpless) from the students. As you will have noted from the case study, the students that Mick is working with are young adults and – like the students you work with – their identity and self-esteem are often fragile as they struggle with their emotional development. As you may well have found when working with your own students, if they feel that you are treating them like children they will give a childish response. This may take the form of feigned indifference, aggression or misbehaviour that is directed towards you or the situation. In telling his students things *over and over again*, telling them what to revise and so on, Mick may feel he is communicating with his students in an adult way by issuing reminders to point them in the right direction. However, his students may not see it that way. His well-meant reminders may well be seen as the nagging voice of a parent and they may react to this perception by giving what Mick sees as childish responses – not turning up or simply giving up on something that they feel is too challenging. We all react to other people and how we think they see us. In the case study students are reacting to how they feel Mick sees them (as children rather than as valued or 'respected' individuals) and this is likely to have a negative impact on their self-image and level of self-esteem.

Critical thinking activity: developing student motivation

From the case study evidence it would seem that the students that Mick is working with have adopted a childlike stance in response to Mick's teaching.

» *Think about Berne's theory of transactional analysis and write down some suggestions about how Mick could use the theory to improve his communication with students.*

To be more effective in the classroom Mick needs to replace his role as a controlling 'parent' with adult-to-adult transactions which will be less likely to trigger a child ego response from students. As you will know from your own experience, all students, particularly those who are in the process of making the transition from adolescence into adulthood, need to feel valued and respected. Young children need positive 'strokes' or signs of recognition and approval from an adult in order to develop emotionally. When children are small these may be given in a physical form such as cuddles or smiles. As they grow, physical actions are exchanged for mental or emotional strokes from parents or teachers, such as praise or expressions of recognition for effort, which stimulate and develop student motivation.

Developing student autonomy

Young students find it difficult to balance their need to feel in control of their actions with their recognition of their position as a student. They have a need to be accepted as independent adults capable of making their own decisions and having control over their learning. However, particularly in the first few months of their course, they are in a dependent relationship with a tutor who controls their access to and relationship with 'consecrated' knowledge (Bourdieu, 1984 in Fowler, 1997), the important recognised facts and knowledge of their chosen subject. One of the strategies you might have suggested that Mick could use is to raise the level of student autonomy within the teaching and learning processes. This can be positive for students as it both includes and values them as individuals; and, as you know, this can be a significant factor in motivating young people. Bandura (1977) suggests that the level of a student's inclusion in learning is determined by their belief in their own abilities to achieve their goals. You as a teacher can have a very strong influence on a student's level of self-belief. The development of innate motivation within the student – a genuine enthusiasm for learning – is central to building their self-esteem. By including the student in the learning process, recognising their competence as a student, developing a productive relationship with them and granting them autonomy to make decisions (albeit within defined parameters), the teacher can promote motivation and achievement.

Identifying what motivates students

Learning to identify what motivates our students has long been recognised by teachers as being central to successful student-centred learning. The work of theorists such as Maslow (1954) or Knowles (1980) is commonly cited in this context. The Merriam Webster Dictionary (online) gives three definitions of motivation, describing it variously as the process of *giving someone a reason for doing something*; the *condition of being eager to act or work* and as a *force or influence that causes someone to do something*. In terms of teaching, therefore, it is clear that your actions as a teacher can influence students' motivation to be included in the learning process. We can help them to want to do something by making it interesting or rewarding (intrinsic motivation) or we can incentivise our students (external motivation) through rewards or sanctions. You will probably agree that it is much easier for a student to learn if they want to do something. Two elements which have been discussed earlier in this chapter can be used by the teacher to generate intrinsic motivation in students – transactional analysis and social learning theory. By using groups (social learning) and group work in tasks and allowing the groups a level of autonomy and independence (treating the students as adults – transactional analysis) the teacher can apply elements of both of these theories as catalysts for learning.

CASE STUDY

The painting and decorating lecturer's tale – working in the workshop

The second part of the supportive observation suggested by Mick's tutor took place with the same group but this time in a workshop setting. The workshop is set out as a row of small 'rooms' which contain all of the elements that the students will have to either paint or decorate to achieve their qualification at different levels: ceilings, door and window frames, architraves, corners, etc.; different surfaces for them to try various prescribed decorative techniques; and two larger demonstration 'rooms' which are more open and designed for the tutors to use for demonstrations. During the discussion afterwards Mick was very honest in his assessment of the situation and made the following comments.

Well, I certainly feel more at home in the workshop than the classroom – something to do with having something practical to teach I suppose. The 'rooms' make it a bit difficult to work at times because you can't see all of them at the same time. In general they seem to be a bit more interested when they are working in here. I give them a demonstration of what they've got to do first, and tell them what to do as I'm showing them, and then they have to go and practise. They are just so needy though, and they take forever to do something unless you are with them all the time, but to be honest, 90 per cent of the time you just have to tell them what to do and how to do it, and do it with them all over again. I've tried getting them to work in groups to do things but the rooms are poky and if there's a group of them they just mess about. They hide in the rooms because they know I can't see them and to be honest they don't get much done. We won't talk about the quality of their work because sometimes there just isn't any; they seem to think that if they've done something once they should move onto something new. They don't seem to understand that 'practice makes perfect'; it's a case of 'good enough will do' with most of them. Anyway, I keep them down to working in pairs, but it's wearing though – I seem to spend all my time rushing from one pair to another to try to keep them on task. They're getting there, but some days it feels like pulling teeth. I'm not getting them to do anything, let alone learn something.

Critical thinking activity: using groups in teaching and learning

Although Mick professes to be more at home in the workshop, he still seems to be facing some challenges in terms of teaching and learning.

» *Read this second case study again and make some notes about how you think Mick could use group work effectively in the workshop.*

Getting the best out of group work

Active learning

> *Learning is something that the pupil has to do himself and for himself, the initiative ... [must lie] ... with the learner. The teacher is a guide and director; he steers the boat but the energy that propels it must come from those who are learning.*
>
> Dewey (1933, in Boydston 2008, p 140)

Your role as a teacher in guiding the learning is critical in developing successful group work techniques, and as with any learning strategy, learning in groups must be a purposeful activity, with clear objectives and realistic but challenging time frames to focus activity. You will have seen from Mick's comments that rather than captaining a single boat full of students he has created a small fleet of dinghies which are sailing in different directions. His students are working in pairs in discrete 'rooms' that are difficult to monitor, and knowing they need significant amounts of attention, he is spending his time *rushing from one pair to another to try to keep them on task* following his demonstration. While the effectiveness of group learning has been widely recognised (Lave and Wenger, 1991; Race, 2000) and young students may wish to be self-directed in their learning, it is entirely possible, at least in the initial stages of their course, that they lack both the subject knowledge and personal maturity to work semi-autonomously in pairs. However, Mick has the option of organising the students into groups rather than pairs and using the larger rooms currently used by tutors for demonstrations as active teaching areas. This would not only make it easier for him to monitor and control his students but also allow him to meet two crucial conditions for effective learning groups in an educational context: a common purpose and social interaction, both of which can be controlled and engineered by the teacher.

Mick, who is already finding it difficult to manage the students in pairs, might initially baulk at the idea of introducing larger groups, preferring instead to continue to work on the divide and rule theory. However, by using some of the principles devised by Belbin (1981) to define individual roles for students within the group he could engineer groups of students to work towards small 'chunked' tasks, and the accomplishment of these would provide students with a sense of achievement and ultimately increase motivation. As you may have found already, getting students to work as groups is not always an easy task. Mick would need to be aware of the difficulties that can arise during the formation of effective learning groups (Tuckman, 1965). He might also have to be prepared to intervene at times and work with his students to help them find ways of working together, but the potential advantages to both the students and the tutor undoubtedly outweigh the difficulties that might be encountered.

Most teachers, and you may be one of them, find group work an effective learning strategy. Our students like being in groups to work through problems, master the basics of content and apply principles in practice rather than having to ask for help from the teacher. Group work can meet our students' need to have some control over their learning, and it frees us to actively manage students' progress rather than simply directing activities. The interaction and co-operation of group work can also significantly decrease the sense of isolation felt by some students, particularly those who find the work difficult or who have a special need of some sort. In groups our students have the opportunity to learn from each other and, by discussing or trialling different solutions to achieve a common goal (which is in itself motivational), they are able to make connections between theory and practice and achieve deep, rather than surface, understanding of theories through applying them in a practical situation. By using a practical task you may also have an opportunity to help students make connections with the wider skills (such as English or mathematics) which are needed for work by showing their use in a practical setting.

All of our students differ in terms of their ability and experience, and group work can offer your more advanced students the opportunity to develop and use higher-level thinking skills (analysis, evaluation and synthesis) through their experience of negotiation, conflict resolution, problem solving and teamwork as the group develops. Experience of working in groups can also provide students with a structured learning experience that prepares them for the workplace by developing social and communication skills, their understanding of the need to work with diverse memberships and the expectations of groups in terms of responsibilities, behaviour, communication and commitment from the individual.

Encouraging peer interaction

Hattie and Timperley (2007) say that one of the most important things that we can do as a teacher is to provide feedback. As you know, when you have a big group of students, giving individual feedback can be a time-consuming task. As well as becoming engaged in the learning process, group work can also offer your students the chance to have their work assessed in different ways. Your students can assess their own work (ipsative, self-reflective assessment) or have their work informally assessed by their peers within the group. As we noted earlier, students can be very sensitive to the power differential between themselves and the tutor, something which is particularly true for those who Ecclestone and Hayes (2009) would describe as having *fragile identities* or who for some reason feel excluded from the learning process. Their already low self-esteem may be reduced even further by criticism (however constructive, well-intentioned and gently given) from the teacher. However, you may find that your less-confident students respond quite differently to peers giving the same type of constructive criticism or explaining something in a different way. It is advisable, though, to negotiate some firm rules with students on the necessity of making feedback and teaching constructive before these particular activities are introduced.

Once group work has been established in the workshop environment Mick should be able to transfer the method into his classroom practice. As many of you know from your own experience, working in a classroom is very different from working in a practical setting, but a lot of the activities that we have looked at in this chapter can be used in both environments. Access to different types of facilities will also allow Mick to include other types of inclusive learning activities such as research-based activities or guided learning in groups. These activities can include peer presentations which will enable students to develop their IT skills as well as promoting levels of self-confidence.

All in all there is a lot to be said for group work!

Conclusion

As we saw above, Dewey reminds us that the role of the teacher in steering the good ship learning is both central and critical to the students' voyage of discovery. Our role as a guide implies leadership but, in addition to conducting the expedition, we also need to build a crew of students, maintaining and developing their confidence and morale, facilitating and scaffolding their progress towards their ultimate goal of successful completion of their chosen course of study.

Chapter reflections

New teachers will find it helpful to keep the following ideas in mind when planning their teaching.

» *Learning is a social activity and most students thrive when they learn co-operatively.*

» *Social learning helps students to 'make meaning' of new knowledge.*

» *The role the teacher adopts in communication with students is critical in establishing their relationship with students.*

» *Understanding students' motivation is key to supporting their learning.*

» *Developing group work can be a difficult process, but it is one that facilitates learning.*

Taking it further

Rogers, A and Horrocks, N (2010) *Teaching Adults*. Milton Keynes: Open University Press.

An accessible book that discusses formal and informal learning and how teachers can facilitate ways of learning.

Wenger, E (1998) *Communities of Practice: Learning, Meaning and Identity*. Cambridge: Cambridge University Press.

A useful and interesting extension of the theory of communities of practice in social learning theory.

References

Bandura, A (1977) *Social Learning Theory*. Englewood Cliffs, NJ: Prentice Hall.

Bartlett, S and Burton, D (2012) *Introduction to Education Studies*. London: Sage.

Belbin, M (1981) *Management Teams: Why They Succeed or Fail*. Oxford: Heinemann Professional Publishing Ltd.

Berne, E (1961) *Transactional Analysis in Psychotherapy: A Systematic Individual and Social Psychiatry*. New York: Grove Press.

Bono, E de (1985) *Six Thinking Hats*. London: Little Brown and Company.

Bruner, J (1996) *The Culture of Education*. Cambridge, Mass.: Harvard University Press.

Butcher, J (2005) *Developing Effective 16–19 Teaching Skills*. Abingdon: RoutledgeFalmer.

Deci, E L, Vallerand, R J, Pelletier, L G and Ryan, R M (1991) Motivation and Education: The Self-Determination Perspective. *The Educational Psychologist*, 26: 325–46.

Dewey, J (2008) in Boydston, J (ed) *The Later Works of John Dewey, Volume 8, 1925–1953: 1933, Essays and How We Think*. London: Macmillan and Co.

Ecclestone, K and Hayes, D (2009) *The Dangerous Rise of Therapeutic Education*. Abingdon: Routledge.

Fowler, B (1997) *Pierre Bourdieu and Cultural Theory: Critical Investigations*. London: Sage.

Freire, P (1972) *Pedagogy of the Oppressed*. Harmondsworth: Penguin.

Hattie, J and Timperley, H (2007) The Power of Feedback. *Review of Educational Research*, 77(1): 81–112.

Jarvis, M (2005) *The Psychology of Effective Learning and Teaching*. Cheltenham: Nelson Thornes.

Knowles, M S (1980) *The Modern Practice of Adult Education. From Pedagogy to Andragogy*. Englewood Cliffs: Prentice Hall/Cambridge.

Kolb, D A (1984) *Experimental Learning Experience as a Source of Learning and Development*. New Jersey: Prentice Hall.

Lave, J and Wenger, E (1991) *Situated Learning: Legitimate Peripheral Participation*. Cambridge: Cambridge University Press.

Maslow, A H (1954) *Motivation and Personality*. New York: Harper and Row.

Race, P (2000) *500 Tips on Group Learning*. London: Kogan Page.

Rosenthal, R and Jacobson, L (1968) *Pygmalion in the Classroom*. New York: Holt, Rinehart & Winston.

Tuckman, B (1965) Developmental Sequence in Small Groups. *Psychological Bulletin*, 63: 384–99.

Young, M and Lucas M (1999) Pedagogy in Further Education: New Contexts, New Theories and New Possibilities in Mortimore, P *Understanding Pedagogy and its Impact on Learning*. London: Paul Chapman Publishing Ltd.

Websites

Merriam Webster Dictionary online (2013). Available at www.merriam-webster.com.

Wenger, E (c 2007) *Communities of Practice. A Brief Introduction*. Available at www.ewenger.com/theory/ (last accessed 14 January 2014).

5 Mainstream mayhem

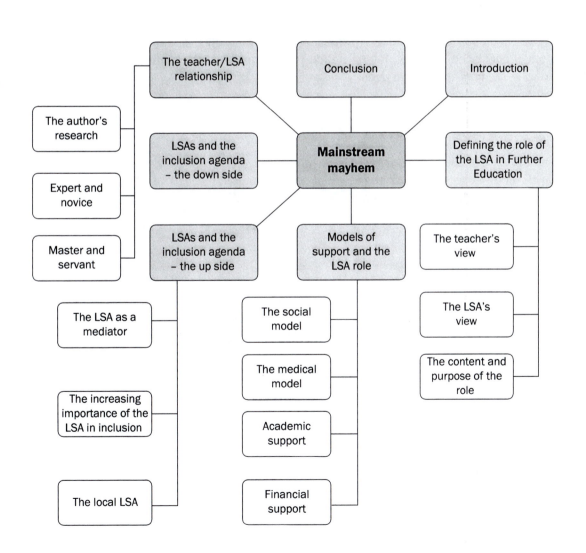

Chapter aims

This chapter investigates the role of Learning Support Assistants (LSAs) in FE. In doing so it considers the external influences on the role of the LSA and the impact that these have on the relationship between the teacher and the LSA in the classroom. The role of the LSA in promoting inclusive practice in the classroom is also discussed and the chapter concludes by exploring areas of potential good practice between teachers and LSAs in the classroom.

Introduction

You may have read Saxe's 1873 poem, 'The Blind Men and the Elephant'. Based on a folk-lore tale from India it shows how six unsighted men from Indostan touch an elephant and then describe their impressions to the others based only on what they have felt. Each of them describes something different: a wall, a spear, a snake, a tree, a fan or a rope, depending on which part of the animal they touched. Unsurprisingly this leads to disagreement as each is convinced that their interpretation is right and the others are wrong. But as Saxe notes in the final lines of the poem:

> *... each was partly in the right,*

> *And all were in the wrong!*

The poem warns us of the danger of making assumptions based on preconceived ideas and partial knowledge. As you will see as you read this chapter, the lessons of this story can well be applied to the way the role of the LSA in FE is understood.

Defining the role of the LSA in Further Education

In theory the role of the LSA should be one that you can easily define; but as you will see as we go through the chapter, that is far from true. The place of the LSA in the classroom, their precise role and their impact on inclusive learning varies from college to college. Before we explore the role of the LSA you need to think about what you already know about it, how you feel about LSAs and what you think their role is in an inclusive classroom.

Critical thinking activity: identifying the role of the LSA

The range of titles and purposes attached to the role of the LSA can have an effect on the way that they are used in a classroom. Read the case study and make some notes on:

» *the different views of the role;*

» *how the different views might impact on teaching and learning.*

CASE STUDY

Jameela

Jameela is a fully trained hairdresser who runs her own salon in partnership with her husband. While working in the salon Jameela trained apprentices on work experience and, when she found that she enjoyed teaching, she decided to train as a teacher at a college of Further Education. After gaining her Cert Ed last year (*the most difficult thing I have ever done – all that writing, all those books!*) she is now in her first year of working as a 0.5 lecturer in hairdressing at the same college. Most of the time she is teaching either apprentices or full-time students at level 2, but she also has a few practical sessions with level 3 students.

Karl

Karl recently graduated from university with a 2:1 in social anthropology and is settling into his first 'proper job'. He wants to train as a secondary school teacher and is working as a support assistant at the college until he can return to university to do his PGCE.

Both Jameela and Karl keep a reflective personal blog in which they detail the day's events.

Jameela's blog

Well, another day at the chalk-face, all the usual problems today, especially with the Level 2 students who are just so needy sometimes. How many times do you have to explain the theory of mixing a colour? Why do they not seem to understand that you need to get the ratios right otherwise it just isn't the shade the client wants? After all the work I put in to the theory class at 9.00 to show them, they still got it wrong in the practical. Thank goodness they were practising on the 'blocks' and not a real customer today, otherwise at least one of them would have walked out with bright pink hair. Honestly, sometimes you need eyes in the back of your head!

To top it all off, Margie, who usually supports me on that lesson, and knows exactly what I want her to do, has to pick today of all days to go sick and I had a right ding-bat in her place who arrived just about at the end of the theory lesson right as they were going to start the practical. Nice enough lad but what did he know about hairdressing? Zilch! What was I supposed to do with him? He didn't even know the students and he didn't have a clue what he was supposed to be doing to help me teach! How do I get it through to the LSA administrator that I need someone who knows what they are doing to work with the difficult ones that need help to keep up and the 'low-achievers'? She just seems to think that any old support in a classroom is enough to get them through the exams now the pressure is really on to make sure that they all pass. Isn't it enough that I have to do all the planning and cope with 16 of them without giving me someone else to look after?

Karl's blog

Great day today –not! Margie was off so the LSA administrator sent me over to cover for her class – hairdressing of all things. Not that I have got anything against hairdressers mind, but a bit of guidance on what I was supposed to have been doing from the teacher wouldn't have gone amiss. It seemed like she just thought I would know what to do. I had had a quick look at Margie's file before I went in and made a couple of notes about the students. I found out that three of them have dyslexia and there was a scribble about 'suspected ADHD', but no indication of who it referred to. Anyway, reading notes about students isn't much good unless someone tells you who they are, is it?

I know learning support is supposed to be about helping the student to be able to learn their vocational skills, but a lot of the work with students is generic and focuses on developing functional and learning skills with a 'good' group, and general behaviour with a 'bad' one. I could really have helped some of them if she had told me that they had been working on ratios in the theory lesson. OK, I know that most of them are likely to be a bit weak in terms of functional skills; that seems to go with the territory. But it would have helped if she had told me how ratios fitted into hairdressing or even told me what she was teaching! Sometimes I want to remind them that I'm an LSA not a mind reader.

The teacher's view

Clearly communication here is a major problem. The role of the LSA in the classroom is viewed very differently by the participants. You will have noticed that both parties feel frustrated and the support that should be available to the students is suffering as a result. Your notes on the case study may show that Jameela's view of the role of the LSA is to support the teacher, rather than the student. She also expects the LSA to have enough subject knowledge to work with groups. You may also feel that she sees her role in the classroom as that of the director or manager of the learning process and that to do this she should be able to delegate her teaching responsibilities for *the difficult ones that need help* to the LSA.

The LSA's view

You will have noted that the LSA sees his role in much more generic terms. His concern is with the individual student and he sees his role as helping students to develop their functional skills by embedding them in the vocational subject. He can't identify the students who he is supposed to be helping and he feels that he is unable to fulfil his role properly.

The content and purpose of the role

Within FE a wide range of technical, specialist and pastoral staff are available to students and teachers, all of whom might be regarded as supporting learning and students in one form or another. Farrell et al. (2010) note that approximately 176,900 staff were employed in schools in 2008 in a learning support role, but as you have seen, the role of the LSA is not always clear. Your own experience may lead you to think that LSAs are mainly there to support the academic work of your students who have been identified as having some form of special need. If you have worked in FE for a while or have worked at different colleges you may also have seen them used in a wider role of *learning mentors*. In this role they may well still be supporting students with their academic work, but they are also supporting them with their personal and social development. The situation is very confusing and, as Robson and Bailey (2008, p 305) note, in practice there is a wide range of titles and variation ... *[in]* ... *tasks* ... *[allocated to the LSA]* ... *between providers* ... *and within individual providers* as the role of the LSA is generally defined by the FE college itself. Although the individual college defines the role to meet their particular needs, there are some external factors which influence the models of support that are available and the way in which LSAs are used, and these are discussed below.

Models of support and the LSA role

Financial support

As with all things, the financial and political aspects of supporting students have to be considered. If you reflect on your personal experience of working as a teacher in FE over the past few years (or if you are new to the sector perhaps you might be able to ask more experienced teachers about this), you may be able to identify changes in funding and policy which have affected the way that learning support is used in your college. At the present time FE colleges can only apply for funding to finance learning support for students who are on government-funded programmes of learning. As many of you who run courses that normally attract older students will have found, those who do not fall into this funding category and are self-funding or being sponsored by employers have no automatic right to learning support. The costs of adult support are borne largely by the FE college itself which, despite not being able to access additional support funding, nevertheless has a statutory obligation to meet the requirements of the Disability and Equality Act 2010.

Changes in compulsory education, the raising of the school-leaving age and the increasing number of academy schools with vocational provision in their sixth forms have increased the competition for students who would previously have come into FE. These changes have also altered the emphasis of the support provided for students in FE. Academic support, given in the classroom to either individuals or groups of students, continues to be a major part of the support role. However, you may have noticed that learning support has become increasingly focused on the pastoral care of students, to enhance the overall 'learning experience' and attract, retain and increase the number of students. The recent requirement for all students to gain GCSE grades at C or above while in education has also diverted support resources into developing students' skills in these areas.

Academic support

Support can take a variety of forms in FE and is provided to help ensure that all students achieve their learning aims. General needs, such as low literacy levels, are frequently addressed through general 'in class' LSA support; and so you may well have had an LSA in your classroom helping one (or more) of your students to meet their academic or vocational aims. You may also have had students with a specific support need, behavioural difficulties or dyslexia who have 'in class' support for a set number of hours in the week. LSA support may be provided for students who are 'failing' in some way, perhaps due to short-term personal or social difficulties, whom staff may feel are at risk of leaving the course. But there are other students in our colleges who need more intensive support. Support isn't always given in the mainstream classroom and you may be able to think of groups or individuals in your college who receive specialised support in the form of focused classes with intense LSA support. These groups may include students with severe or multiple learning difficulties, those who are not yet ready to begin a mainstream qualification, or those with English as a Second or Other Language (ESOL) for example. The common strand in support for all of these students is that it is provided to meet a specific need, a deficiency which is preventing the student from achieving their full potential.

The medical model

The medical model is based on the notion of *deficit*, the idea that the student is lacking in some way. This drives the approach when setting up support. The student is seen as being vulnerable and as having a difficulty that needs some form of treatment, but their difficulty is seen as personal – as part of them as a person. You may have students in your class with ADHD or dyslexia for example. These are difficulties that are assumed to be 'their' difficulty. LSA help for students who have a difficulty that is 'their problem' often lasts throughout the student's time in FE and is often one of the most important factors in enabling the student to be included in mainstream learning.

The social model

As a teacher in FE you may also have worked with students who are vulnerable, disengaged or under-achieving but who do not have a difficulty which is 'located within the person' and are not achieving for other reasons. They may have social, emotional or behavioural difficulties that result from their social background. You may have already worked with students who lack confidence or have poor social or communication skills which sometimes lead to poor or challenging behaviour. Their difficulties are not medical, but they are real, and they make it difficult for them to take part in mainstream learning. One of the elements of the hidden curriculum which underpins much of the work that we do in FE is building self-confidence, self-esteem and social skills as part of students' preparation for work and life. As we will see in other parts of this book, your empathy and understanding of social difficulties and the ways in which you work in the classroom to help your students to overcome these difficulties, play a very important part in supporting students and helping them to achieve.

Critical thinking activity: a medical or social perspective?

Re-read the blog entries made by Jameela and Karl.

» *Do their views reflect any of the factors we have just discussed?*

LSAs and the inclusion agenda – the up side

Whether the support your students receive is generated by academic or social needs it is all part of FE's inclusive student-centred approach and the support is intended to ensure that your students are able to succeed in their learning. FE, like every other sector in education, is under pressure to make sure that its students remain on the course and complete their qualifications successfully. As a consequence, LSA support is becoming increasingly focused on supporting the academic needs of the students. Indeed, Tews and Lupart (2008) suggest that there is a general assumption within FE that the use of LSAs will always improve student outcomes. With the additional pressure to ensure that their students achieve, many teachers – and this may include you – feel that their role in the classroom has changed over the past few years and that in addition to teaching they have also become a manager of the learning process. They have become responsible for the *direction* of learning in addition to delivering *differentiated* learning; and so for them the LSA's role in the classroom has become increasingly important. By delegating the support of those who need it most to LSAs so that they themselves can concentrate on the majority, teachers are more able to meet the needs of all students.

The increasing importance of the LSA in inclusion

You may remember from the case study that Jameela organised her class so that the LSA worked with the 'difficult' or 'low-level' students. You might feel that this indicates that she has adopted the role of a manager in the classroom. In other words, it may suggest to you that she is less engaged with those students and has a more distant relationship with them. I would hasten to add that I am not in any way suggesting that she is uncaring. However, it seems that LSAs have become increasingly responsible for assuming one of the principal burdens of inclusion within the classroom – the *emotional labour* (Colley, 2006, p 16) of meeting the social, academic and emotional interaction of students who are in need of support.

The local LSA

Many writers, (for example, Lacey, 2001; Downing et al., 2000; Gerschel, 2005) have commented on the role of the LSA as a positive force for inclusion. If you look around your staffroom you may well see that many of the teachers are not 'natives' of the locale in which they teach and their views of the world and of teaching have often been shaped by their experience in Higher Education. The LSAs that you work with, on the other hand, may be working mothers, living close to the school environment, whose local knowledge of the area helps them to relate to your students and support them. They understand where your students are 'coming from' socially and often economically, and they also have a good understanding of the local education system and of FE itself. The combination of these factors means that they can often 'reach out' to students in a way that teachers cannot. They can use their local knowledge to empathise with the position of your students, but also help to include them in the college and in the classroom by acting as a mediator, explaining the needs and requirements of FE to the student, and the student's needs to the teacher and institution. By offering empathic support at an emotional and social level they can often play a critical role in retaining less-confident students or students with social challenges in FE.

The LSA as a mediator

Used effectively, your LSA can become a very effective mediator in the classroom. Working as the 'go-between' connecting you and your students, they can work with students to build on their existing knowledge and skills, helping them to make sense and create meaning from your teaching. That is not to say that you are not teaching effectively or differentiating, but in an inclusive classroom some of your students may need extra help. By modifying your instruction and further differentiating your materials, LSAs can make learning more accessible for these students. Another critical part of their role is in developing the personal skills of your students: working with others, communication, personal independence and empowerment. Although many LSAs are employed to support a specific student, you may also find that they can play a very positive role in developing group work in your classroom. By initially supporting individual students in group work the LSA is facilitating the inclusion of the individual in the social activity of your classroom, adding to their sense of 'belonging' and developing their self-esteem (Maslow, 1954). You may find quite quickly that the role of the LSA in the group changes from individual support to group support, encouraging the development of wider skills of teamwork and communication between the students.

From this perspective the LSA has a significant role in including the student in both the formal and informal learning of the classroom, facilitating inclusion by developing their understanding of the educational space to allow them to interact effectively with other students and the teacher. Through empathic, structured support, based on knowledge of the social, cultural and personal values, beliefs and traditions of the individual student, the LSA is able to facilitate the transfer of social and emotional knowledge in addition to academic knowledge.

LSAs and the inclusion agenda – the down side

If you have a look at the literature on LSAs you will find that most of it emphasises the positive aspects of their role. However, over the past few years there have been a growing number of writers who are considering the possibility that the level of support in FE is too great and can be intrusive. Ecclestone (2004), for example, suggests that over supporting students can lead to students being 'diminished' through becoming dependent on support and developing a form of learned helplessness, seeing themselves as unable to learn effectively without support.

A somewhat different view of inclusion and the role of the LSA in the inclusion process is offered by Ernst-Slavit and Wenger (2006) who concentrate on the role of the LSA in persuading students to conform to the expectations of the institution, working with them to develop the 'correct' or expected responses in terms of academic, social and attitudinal behaviour towards learning. Somewhat controversially, from this point of view the position of the LSAs can be seen as simply a means of retaining students who fall below the expected standards in some way and who, without help, would be excluded from education. It is also possible to suggest that if LSA support is used ineffectively, then rather than including students they have the potential to create barriers between the supported students and the rest of the class and devalue those with additional needs in the eyes of their peers.

Critical thinking activity: your own situation

Take a few minutes to think about your own position, that of your colleagues and also that of your institution in relation to the purpose and impact of LSAs in the classroom.

» *Is the focus of the LSA role to develop academic standards or to include students in the wider aspects of education?*

» *What evidence have you got for this?*

» *Is the focus something that you would like to change, and if so how would you do so?*

The teacher/LSA relationship

At the beginning of this chapter you will remember reading Karl and Jameela's blogs and thinking about the differences in the ways they saw the role of the LSA. Throughout the chapter we have looked at different explanations for their views, but we have not as yet developed any strategies for improving the situation. If you look back over your notes for the critical thinking exercise you will remember that there were a number of areas of misunderstanding:

- the confused perceptions of the role of the LSA held by each;

- the relative roles of the teacher and the LSA;

- the importance of communication;

- the importance of continuity;

- the importance of identifying the boundaries of actions within the classroom.

We have already looked at the different perceptions of the role of the LSA in FE, the importance of communication, boundaries and continuity. So in the next section we'll look at the remaining element: the personal and professional relationship that exists between you as the teacher and the LSA in the classroom. Quicke (2003) identifies two key types of potential relationship: the *master and servant* relationship and the *expert and novice* relationship.

Master and servant

In this relationship you as the teacher would be seen to be the dominant force, organising learning and having responsibility for the achievement of learning outcomes. The role of the LSA in your classroom would become that of a servant, being directed and monitored by you in a relationship which is focused on the teaching rather than the learning process.

Expert and novice

Here the relationship between you and your LSA is seen as more of a partnership or co-operative approach. The learning outcomes for the students are known by both parties; and the LSA, although guided by the teacher, has a level of autonomy in terms of making decisions about the way the information is passed on to the student. Both the teacher and the LSA are actively involved in the teaching and learning processes. In this inclusive environment the focus remains on student achievement, but the LSA is empowered in their work with the students.

The author's research

My own research with LSAs in an FE setting involved me in some fairly lengthy interviews with staff and LSAs. When I analysed the results it was clear that what the LSAs really valued was communication and being involved in the learning process. Their main concern was to ensure that they were able to help 'their' students effectively. Another concern was the need to help 'their' students keep up with their peers in terms of work rate. All of the LSAs in this study talked about the need to communicate with the teacher. They felt that communication with the teacher (and sometimes other LSAs) about the students they were supporting and about the subject that they were 'translating' (the LSA's description) for 'their' student was critical in order for them to be able to support students effectively. As one of them said:

> *I know the students but sometimes the subject is a bit of a mystery. Sometimes I'm supporting in art and other times in engineering and I don't always know what the teacher is talking about which makes it tricky when I want to find a way of explaining something or helping them understand how to do something – sometimes I feel like I could do with a bit of support myself!*

One of the key findings that came out of this research was that where there was a co-operative relationship with teachers in the classroom, founded on mutual respect and trust, communication did not become an issue. The LSAs recognised that the teachers were busy, but all of them felt that if they were prepared for their role by just *touching base ... [with the teacher] ... at the start of the lesson* for the lesson outline and key objectives and so on, and at the end of it for feedback, they would be much better able to help their students. Several of them also thought it would be useful if the teacher could give them advance warning of what they would be doing in the lesson *just in case I need to brush up a bit on something* as one of them told me, and to help them to plan future support more effectively.

The LSAs in this study also wanted feedback from the teacher on what they were doing in the lesson, which would seem to confirm Devlin's (2008) findings. The feedback that they most appreciated was part of a two-way process focused on learning and the student. As they worked more closely with the student they felt that they were in a good position to feed back on 'their' student's progress and any difficulties they were having with the work and progress towards their individual learning goals. They also felt that their relationship with the student often gave them access to information about difficulties or sometimes personal circumstances that were affecting the learning. While not wanting to break any confidences, they wanted to make sure that the teacher was 'in the loop' if these were causing behavioural or academic issues. Also noted were any specific difficulties that the student had experienced or other details about behaviour that needed to be brought to the teacher's attention.

Keeping everyone informed

As you will remember from reading the case study, Karl was 'covering' a class for an absent colleague. Just as you would sometimes find it difficult at short notice to take a class you have not worked with before, LSAs find it difficult to do their job effectively with very little prior warning or information. Karl had tried to find out about the difficulties that the students he was about to work with might be experiencing in the classroom; but, as you may have found from your own experience, any break in continuity in terms of support staff leads to a disruption in routine for the teacher, the LSA and the students. The LSAs I spoke to stressed the importance of communication with staff; so you might like to think about introducing a form that the LSA can fill in at the end of the lesson to record progress (and behaviour where appropriate) which could be passed on should LSA cover be required. You might also find that temporary or new LSAs can get 'up to speed' and function more effectively if they are able to access the Individual Learning Plans (ILPs) that are maintained by the students and in which they record their objectives and achievements on a daily basis.

The importance of guidelines

After a few lessons you will have got to know your students and will know how they should be 'handled' so that they get the best from your teaching. Although all FE colleges have policy documents which detail acceptable and unacceptable behaviour, as teachers we sometimes have to interpret these to suit the class we are working with. For example, the behaviour that you would expect from an A level group is likely to be very different from what you would expect from a group of NEETs students. As one of the LSAs I spoke to noted, *Teachers are all a bit different in what they allow* in terms of behaviour. You may know what behaviours you allow in the classroom, but a new or temporary LSA won't, and you will need to make sure that your LSA knows what you do and do not allow students to do or say. Clear guidelines about behaviour which the students are aware of and which the teacher enforced are, to quote one LSA, *an absolute godsend*. In the case study Karl had no awareness of the boundaries that the teacher had established and this put him at a disadvantage: if he was too stern the students would complain and if he was too lax the teacher would think him ineffective – a no-win situation. LSAs, like all of us, work more efficiently if they know what is expected of them!

Critical thinking activity: improving the situation

Think about the points made above and consider your teaching, your current working relationship with LSAs or any LSA-supported classes you have observed.

»   *What could be done to improve the working relationship with the LSA?*

»   *How can the LSA be helped to make the learning process more effective?*

Conclusion

As you will have noticed as you have read the chapter, there are many competing views on the precise role of the LSA in terms of content and responsibilities. What is clear is that although the role is deeply embedded within the FE system, LSAs are frequently one of the most undervalued resources in the classroom, and are all too often seen as the teacher's assistant rather than the student's aide. However, if you work with them effectively in the classroom, they are potentially a powerful tool for inclusion. As they are ideally positioned to work to advance the academic skills of the student, you will find that they also have the opportunity to work with students to cultivate their personal, social and behavioural skills to develop confident, well-rounded students able to take their place in wider society. After all – isn't that the real purpose of education?

Chapter reflections

This chapter has highlighted:

» the difficulty in determining the content and purpose of the role of the LSA in FE due to the lack of uniformity;

» the range of types of support that the LSA may be called upon to supply;

» the influence of the medical and social models of support on the role of the LSA;

» the centrality of the relationship between the LSA and the teacher in developing the inclusive classroom;

» the role of the LSA in developing inclusive practice in the classroom and beyond;

» the danger of developing a 'culture of dependency' on LSA support amongst 'vulnerable students';

» the importance of clear roles, responsibilities, boundaries and communication between the teacher and the LSA in using support effectively to include all students in the learning process.

Taking it further

Bailey, B and Robson, J (2004) Learning Support Workers in Further Education in England: a Hidden Revolution? *Journal of Further and Higher Education*, 28(4): 373–93.

Ecclestone, K and Hayes, D (2009) *The Dangerous Rise of Therapeutic Education*. Abingdon: Routledge.

Giangreco, M, Suter, J and Doyle, M (2010) Paraprofessionals in Inclusive Schools: A Review of Recent Research. *Journal of Educational and Psychological Consultation*, 20: 41–57.

Robson, J and Bailey, B (2009) 'Bowing from the Heart': an Investigation into Discourses of Professionalism and the Work of Caring for Students in Further Education. *British Educational Research Journal*, 35(1): 99–117.

References

Abbott, L, McConkey, R and Dobbins, M (2011) Key Players in Inclusion: are We Meeting the Professional Needs of Learning Support Assistants for Pupils with Complex Needs? *European Journal of Special Needs Education*, 2(26): 215–31.

Bailey, B and Robson, J (2004) Learning Support Workers in Further Education in England: a Hidden Revolution? *Journal of Further and Higher Education*, 28(4): 373–93.

Colley, H (2006) Learning to Labour with Feeling: Class, Gender and Emotion in Childcare Education and Training. *Contemporary Issues in Early Childhood*, 7(1): 15–29. Available at http://dx.doi.org/10.2304/ciec.2006.7.1.15 (last accessed 16 February 2012).

Devlin, P (2008) Create Effective Teacher-Paraprofessional Teams. *Intervention in School and Clinic*, 4(1): 41–4.

Downing, J, Ryndak, D and Clark, D (2000) Paraeducators in Inclusive Classrooms: Their Own Perceptions. *Remedial and Special Education*, 21: 171–81.

Ecclestone, K (2004) Learning or Therapy? The Demoralisation of Education. *British Journal of Educational Studies*, 52(2): 112–37.

Ecclestone, K and Hayes, D (2009) *The Dangerous Rise of Therapeutic Education*. Abingdon: Routledge.

Ernst-Slavit, G and Wenger, K (2006) Teaching in the Margins: The Multifaceted Work and Struggles of Bilingual Paraeducators. *Anthropology and Education Quarterly*, 37(1): 62–82.

Farrell, P (2001) Special Education in the Last 20 Years: Have Things Really Got Better? *British Journal of Special Education*, 28(1): 3–9.

Farrell, P, Alborz, A, Howes, A and Pearson, D (2010) The Impact of Teaching Assistants on Improving Pupils' Academic Achievement in Mainstream Schools: a Review of the Literature. *Educational Review*, 62(4): 435–8.

Gerschel, L (2005) The Special Educational Needs Coordinator's Role in Managing Teaching Assistants: The Greenwich Perspective. *Support for Learning*, 20(2): 69–76.

Giangreco, M, Edelman, S, Luiselli, T and MacFarland, S (1997) Helping or Hovering? Effects of Instructional Assistant Proximity on Students with Disabilities. *Exceptional Children*, 64(1): 7–18.

Giangreco, M, Suter, J and Doyle, M (2010) Paraprofessionals in Inclusive Schools: A Review of Recent Research. *Journal of Educational and Psychological Consultation*, 20: 41–57.

Groom, B. (2006) Building Relationships for Learning: The Developing Role of the Teaching Assistant. *Support for Learning*, 21(4): 199–203.

Hancock, R and Eyres, I (2004) Implementing a Required Curriculum Reform: Teachers at the Core, Teaching Assistants on the Periphery? *Westminster Studies in Education*, 27(2): 223–35.

Lacey, P (2001) The Role of Learning Support Assistants in the Inclusive Learning of Pupils with Severe and Profound Learning Difficulties. *Educational Review*, 53(2): 157–67.

Maslow, A (1954) *Motivation and Personality*. New York: Harper Row.

Quicke, J (2003) Teaching Assistants: Students or Servants? *FORUM*, 45(2): 72–74. Available at http://dx.doi.org/10.2304/forum.2003.45.2.10 (last accessed 16 February 2012).

Robson, J and Bailey, B (2008) Learners' Emotional and Psychic Responses to Encounters with Learning Support in Further Education and Training. *British Journal of Educational Studies*, 56(3): 304–22.

Robson, J and Bailey, B (2009) 'Bowing from the Heart': An Investigation into Discourses of Professionalism and the Work of Caring for Students in Further Education. *British Educational Research Journal*, 35(1): 99–117.

Saxe, J G (1992) The Blind Man and the Elephant, in Gardner, M (ed) *Best Remembered Poems*. New York: Dover Publications.

Tews, L and Lupart, J (2008) Students With Disabilities: Perspectives of the Role and Impact of Paraprofessionals in Inclusive Education Settings. *Journal of Policy and Practice in Intellectual Disabilities*, 5(1): 36–46.

Veck, W (2009) From an Exclusionary to an Inclusive Understanding of Educational Difficulties and Educational Space: Implications for the Learning Support Assistant's Role. *Oxford Review of Education*, 35(1): 41–56.

YPLA (2010) *Funding Guidance 2010/11: Additional Learning Support*. Coventry: YPLA.

6 Label literacy

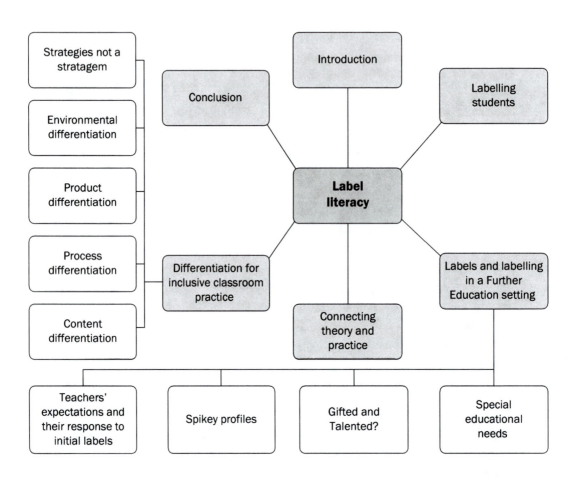

Strategies not a stratagem

Environmental differentiation

Product differentiation

Process differentiation

Content differentiation

Conclusion

Introduction

Labelling students

Label literacy

Differentiation for inclusive classroom practice

Connecting theory and practice

Labels and labelling in a Further Education setting

Teachers' expectations and their response to initial labels

Spikey profiles

Gifted and Talented?

Special educational needs

Chapter aims

Every one of us goes through life wearing labels of some sort. Some of them are positive ('hard worker' or 'likeable'), others are negative ('difficult' or 'moody'). Most of the time the labels don't affect us greatly and some we may just laugh off, but there are times when to be given a label is more serious, and the application of labels to students in FE is one of these times. This chapter sets out to help you to understand the importance of labels in FE by examining the impact of the label on the teacher and the student. It also helps you to explore the meaning of some of the labels that are given to students and how teachers can use their expertise to enable students to challenge any negative labels they may carry with them.

Introduction

I come from a family of 'puzzlers'. Ever since I can remember I have been surrounded by puzzles: jigsaw puzzles, crossword puzzles, mathematical puzzles, logic puzzles ... and by people who can solve them with apparently little or no effort. As I grew older I gradually came to realise that this ability to solve puzzles appeared in some way to be connected with intelligence – which gave me a problem because I couldn't do them. Even when people explained to me how to find the answer to puzzles I still couldn't really see how they had worked it all out, and while I was good in other areas, reading and crafts, this inability to do what everyone else did so easily made me feel different. I passed the 'intelligence test' of the eleven-plus (just, and it was a long time ago!) and made it to the grammar school, but this 'thing' about not being able to do puzzles and its connection with intelligence continued to haunt me and make me feel inferior to those who could do them. By the time I completed my A levels I had just come to think of myself as not being as bright as my peers (and the headmaster had told me that I *wasn't university material* – something that confirmed my opinion of myself). So I was happy to gain a place at a polytechnic while my friends headed off to university. Not making it to university but gaining that place at a 'poly' was possibly the best thing that ever happened to me because I discovered the social sciences, and in particular sociology. It didn't matter that you couldn't solve a logic puzzle in this discipline – you weren't expected to! What mattered was that you could understand ideas, make connections and apply them to the real world – and I could do that! Very gradually I came to realise that my mind was wired to work holistically, to cope with abstract concepts rather than finite puzzles and to use deductive rather than inductive logic. I wasn't unintelligent after all! My brain just didn't work in the way the education system I had experienced up to that point expected it to.

My wandering into the social sciences library one afternoon because the language library was full was pure serendipity. Had I not picked up the book lying on the desk (and quickly abandoned the essay I was supposed to be doing in favour of reading something that eventually led to me switching to sociology) I would have continued to think of myself as unintelligent and inferior to other people. Now, if someone who is (relatively, although possibly not conventionally!) intelligent can be influenced so easily by the labels they make for themselves or which have been given to them by other people, what do you think the likely impact would be of a label for someone who isn't fortunate enough to find something that convinces them that they're just different, not stupid? What do you think happens to young people who leave compulsory education wearing a label that does not describe their real abilities? What do you think happens to students whose talents are not recognised or are simply ignored by 'the system'? The purpose of this chapter is to look at the impact that labels have on young people and their perception of themselves, and the impact of labels on teachers and on teaching and learning.

Labelling students

The influence of norms in developing society's judgement of individuals as different or deviant in some way has been discussed elsewhere in this book. Labels are markers of difference that social groups create by making rules which, when applied, mark particular people as outsiders. A label is not something which is neutral; it is created by powerful individuals and given to the less powerful. Each label is a judgement of the person or group to whom they are applied and has a set of either expectations or behaviours associated with it. Within education, labels can be particularly important to students and to staff. If a student is described as 'intelligent' or 'hard working' you might expect a student who will apply themselves and work hard in class; equally if their behaviour has been labelled as 'good' you may well expect them to be well behaved. However, if a student is described as having 'special needs', being 'lazy' or 'disruptive' then you might have quite a different set of expectations of that student.

Sometimes the judgements that inform our initial opinions of students are based on information we receive from other sources. When students enter FE they bring with them 'hard' information, school reports, statements of need, references from teachers, etc. This is added to during the interview process and induction period using information collected from formal assessments in English and mathematics, and informal staff observation. These judgements are used to channel students *along various routes depending upon the assessment the institution has made* of them (Rist, in Sadovnik et al., 2001, p 153). So before we have even met our students it is quite possible that our opinion of them has begun to be formed, and will have already received labels – for example, in the form of the level and type of qualification that they will be undertaking.

Labels can also come from other sources and in your experience as a teacher you will have heard young people applying labels to each other and seen the effects. A student labelled as a 'swat', a 'nerd' or 'boss' by other students can quickly begin to live up to the label as it becomes a part of their self-concept. Tannenbaum (1938, p 21) argues that if a person is labelled in some way they have *been tagged ... [and] ... [t]he person becomes the thing he is described as being*. This is particularly true of impressionable young people like the ones that you work with who have not yet fully developed a fixed identity or who have low self-esteem.

Other students, teachers and even FE itself apply labels to students. These can be given consciously as is the case with peers who give 'names' to other students; unconsciously through placing students in a particular class or level of qualification (A levels and NVQ awards carry very different expectations of students); or subconsciously by teachers. And you may have found yourself labelling a student either on received information or from your own experience. The danger of labelling is real. If a student is aware of the label they carry with them in education it has the potential to become a 'master label', shaping their journey into adulthood as they set out to achieve the standards (high or low) that other people attach to it. If a teacher is aware of the label attached to a student it may influence the way that they work with them.

Critical thinking activity: the power of a label

Read the three case studies below which show some initial information about three students about to enter a BTEC course in media studies in FE. Then write down your thoughts about:

» *the types of labels these students may have been given;*

» *the possible impact of the label on the student.*

CASE STUDY

The initial information

Bob is a media lecturer at an FE college who is just about to complete the first year of the Cert Ed qualification and is due to meet his class for the first time. Before going into the lesson he has looked at the information in the student files and identified three students to whom he feels he needs to pay particular attention.

Sarah: Sarah did not do well in her GCSEs, achieving passes in art, ILT, CDT, humanities and media studies. Her highest grade (a grade B) was in art, but her other grades were a mixture of Ds and Es. She has had one-to-one LSA support throughout her school career and is statemented. From time to time she suffers from selective mutism, an anxiety disorder in which a person who is normally capable of speech does not speak in specific situations or to specific people. She would like to work 'behind the scenes' in broadcasting.

Qasir: Qasir has gained ten GCSEs in English, mathematics, ILT, French, art, humanities, combined science, German, cultural studies and media studies. He makes very little effort academically, although he excels in both media studies and English. Although he has passed all of his GCSEs (with B and C grades) he could have achieved A or A* grades had his course work not let him down. He has been disruptive in school at times and has become something of a leader in a small group of students who 'play the teachers up' in some lessons. He does not have a clear career path and has decided to do media studies at college and possibly go to university.

James: James is a very practical student. He demonstrates a great deal of ability in CDT and ILT where he got A grades in his GCSEs, but he is weak in both English and mathematics in which he achieved an F and D grade respectively. He has four other GCSEs at grade C including media studies and would like to be a games designer.

Labels and labelling in a Further Education setting

Some, none, or all of the different labels you have identified could be attached to the students in the case study, and you may well have met students like these already when teaching what is now seen as a 'fairly normal' class in FE. You may think that Sarah has the label of 'special needs', whereas you may well have attached the label of a 'spikey profile' student to James as he had gained A grades in some areas and F grades in others. Qasir? Well, students like Qasir are sometimes misjudged. You may well have labelled him as 'disruptive', but there is always the possibility he was simply bored at school as the work wasn't challenging enough to keep him engaged. In an inclusive environment all students should be treated and included within the learning process according to their abilities and needs; but all too frequently, as we noted earlier, the relationship between the teacher, the student and the learning process is tainted by the pernicious influence of a label. In order to challenge labels we need to understand them, so the next section explores one or two of the common labels you might have met as a teacher, and one you might not have associated with students in FE.

Special educational needs

Under the new Code of Practice (2014) special educational needs (SEN) are grouped into four main categories:

*   communication and interaction;
*   cognition and learning;
*   social, mental and emotional health;
*   sensory and/or physical.

Under the Code the FE college has to ensure that the student is placed on the appropriate course and must also ensure there is a named person to co-ordinate SEN support. The support that the college provides will be determined by the type of special need itself, and it is likely that much of the support provided will continue to be in the form of in-class support supplied by Learning Support Assistants (LSAs), or given by the teachers themselves. Most teachers in FE are aware of the SEN label and you may well have gained a good deal of knowledge about different types of special needs and know the types of support that are required. You may already be working with LSAs to support particular needs and you will certainly already be differentiating in your lessons to suit more general, but still important, support needs for other students. However, SEN is a spectrum label which also includes a group rarely considered in FE – that of the Gifted and Talented students.

Gifted and talented?

The government's definition of 'Gifted and Talented' has changed over the past few years. Originally it comes from the era of selective education when IQ (intelligence quotient) tests were used to select those who would attend a grammar school. If a student had a result of 130+ in the IQ test then the student was seen to be gifted, but if they scored only 129 then they were not. So IQ tests were something of a blunt instrument! Definitions have changed since the days of the grammar school/secondary modern divide and a further category – that of being 'talented' – has been added. Using government (2007) definitions, the term 'gifted' was used to describe students who showed academic ability beyond that expected of their peers in one or more subjects. However, talented students were those who had *the ability to excel in practical skills, such as sport, leadership, artistic performance* (DCSF, 2007, p 85).

When I talked to colleagues about including this section one of them said, *Why are you including that? We don't have Gifted and Talented in FE*. I'm not sure I agree. Some high-fliers may prefer the freedom of FE to sixth forms! So you might encounter students in FE who are 'gifted' or 'academically more able' (the terms were revised again in 2012 and the description 'academically more able pupils' is now used). However, the possibility of you working with students who meet the criteria for being 'talented' in FE is considerably higher. This is especially true if you think about students in vocational skills areas whose talents are not catered for by the standard curriculum and have, therefore, gone unnoticed during their time in compulsory education but who shine in FE.

Spikey profiles

Many of the students who could be seen as talented in vocational areas come into FE with what is known as a 'spikey profile' in terms of their academic ability. Their academic skills, often those associated with functional skills, are patchy; in some areas they are better than their peers but in other areas they are behind them. Sometimes this is associated with a specific learning difficulty such as dyslexia or autistic spectrum disorder (ASD), but this is not always the case. You may well be working with students who just have a barrier in terms of learning a particular subject or subjects – how often as teachers have we heard the phrase 'can't do maths' (or some other subject) from a student? Unfortunately, education in FE has become increasingly focused on the ability of students to apply functional skills to decide the level of course (vocational or academic) they can attend. As a result you may well have students with a spikey profile in your class who have been placed on a level of qualification that is below their general ability level. Young people who have recently come to the UK, for example, may have language skills that do not reflect their real or previous academic attainment; or students may have the practical ability to follow the apprenticeship route but are unable to access vocational courses at level 2 or 3 as they lack skills in mathematics or English.

Critical thinking activity: the effects of the label on the teacher

Critically reflect on your own feelings about the labels discussed above.

» *How do you react to students who fall into these categories?*

» *How do you think your attitude towards a label affects your interactions with the student?*

Teachers' expectations and their response to initial labels

Most of us in the early stages of working with a new class have little information about our students and rely on the amalgamation of the facts gathered during the interview and assessment processes. This can colour our assumptions about what can or cannot be expected of the student, and may in turn subconsciously affect our behaviour towards the student. Like all teachers you may have high expectations of students who have a positive label and unconsciously reward them with 'warm fuzzies' (positive 'strokes' or reinforcement as described in transactional analysis theory – see chapter 4). Giving this type of reward can lead to students being more motivated and a having a more positive self-image. In turn this reaction reinforces the teacher's opinion of the rightness of the label of 'good' when considering that student. Conversely, if a negative label of 'special needs', 'behavioural difficulties' or just 'lazy' has been attached to a student you may find that you have lower expectations of them and might, quite unconsciously, use 'cold pricklies' (negative 'strokes' or negative reinforcement) more often than 'warm fuzzies' when working with them. Labelling theory suggests that this will have a negative impact on the self-concept of the student and their behaviour as they try to live up (or down!) to their label; and again this can reinforce initial opinions. What begins as a subjective (and possibly misinformed) label can start to take on an objective dimension as you and other teachers use your unconscious understanding of the labels *in terms of … teaching time … use of praise and control, and the extent of autonomy within the classroom* (Rist in Sadovnik et al., 2001, p 153).

Critical thinking activity: moving students forward

» *Read the case study below and jot down some ideas about the sort of project Bob could devise which would include and engage his 'labelled' students. If you are familiar with theories of learning, such as behaviourism, cognitivism or humanism, you may find it useful to draw on these. If you are not, you'll have the opportunity to reflect on how your ideas fit with these key theories when we discuss them in the next section.*

CASE STUDY

Scaffolding learning

Bob's students have now settled down into their new environment and have completed the first part of the course. The criteria for the module on editing which they are about to start requires them to edit footage that they have filmed to meet the requirements of an advertising brief for a 'customer'. They have to edit it and give a rationale for the way in which this has been done. Bob wants to set up a project for them that will enable students to develop their skills and receive critical formative feedback before he sets the summative assignment later in the module.

During the preceding few weeks he has kept a careful eye on Sarah, James and Qasir and has made the following observations.

Sarah: Very quiet and doesn't mix. Happy to work on her own but gets very stressed out by small group work and won't participate. Is developing basic media skills but lacks confidence and gets a bit flakey when confronted with new software. Has a good eye for design.

Qasir: Bright lad. When he decides to do something he is really good, but keeping him engaged is tough. He picks up theory and abstract ideas like lightning. Very good at concepts, but practical skills are a bit wobbly. Can't be bothered to practise things and gets bored very quickly if he is not busy or has to do the same thing more than a couple of times. Bit of a daydreamer.

James: Methodical and pedantic in his work. Very talented in practical work and really excels in video. Does not work well with theory. Says he can't see the point of it and he can't understand it – only wants to work with practical elements of media. Hard going!

Connecting theory and practice

Renzulli (1998 in Goodhew, 2009) suggests that there are three factors to be considered in stimulating and retaining the interest of the student: ability levels, creativity and commitment. From the notes that Bob has made you may have noted that he is fully aware that the levels of the three 'labelled' students are different in each of these key areas. However, he needs to include them in the exercise that he has to plan in order to meet the unit criteria. He refers back to information on learning theory from the Cert Ed to help him to work out how to meet their needs.

Planning the unit

As with all learning, the students are intended to make progress in the three key areas: the knowledge, skills and attitudes (KSA) associated with the subject matter. You may feel that with careful structuring these elements can be moved forward on three separate but connected continua:

* the movement from easy to challenging in terms of the subject matter;

* the transition from teacher- to student-led in terms of control; and

* the progression from informal formative assessment to formal summative assessment.

All of these can be achieved through careful planning of strategies and interventions designed to scaffold learning. You might have suggested that one of the first things to do is to review the existing scheme of work (SoW) for the unit to check that these movements along the different continua are in place.

Bloom's Taxonomy

One of the key tools that most of us use when working out learning objectives is *Bloom's Taxonomy* (1956). This classification can help you to identify the key stages of progression in each of the three domains of learning (KSA). A number of authors (for example, Clemson, 2013; Reece and Walker, 2007) have devised detailed lists of action verbs associated with each stage of the three domains which you may well find helpful in designing projects or lesson objectives. By using the various verbs you can set objectives that focus on the core content of the lesson and also plan differentiated objectives. Setting objectives for some, most, or all of your students enables all of them to access the learning at a level appropriate to their skills and knowledge. By differentiating objectives and using the action verbs which match the different stages in the domains – asking your students to *recall* information, *identify* differences, *compare* ideas, or *evaluate* facts about the same subject matter – you are ensuring that all of your students are included at the level which is best suited to them. So for example in hairdressing, your student could be asked to *recall* information about the biological construction of a hair by labelling a diagram. You could ask a more advanced student to *compare* hair that has been treated in different ways (permed or coloured, etc.) to show how hair has been changed by treatment. By setting objectives that are accessible but also challenging and stretching you can stimulate and engage more advanced or able students.

Delivering the unit

There are many different schools of thought that inform delivery (and many books devoted to the theory of education), but the three approaches with which you are most likely to be familiar are behaviourism, cognitivism/constructivism and humanism. You might have suggested that a combination of these approaches will help Bob ensure that all his students, including the 'labelled' students, are fully included.

Behaviourism

The key points about behaviourism are that:

*   it is concerned with observable changes in behaviour – so students are seen to have learned if they can repeat an action or fact;

*   it uses rewards and sanctions to encourage compliance;

*   teachers instruct students but students are passive – they are not actively involved in learning;

*   students learn only what they are taught.

Many teachers in FE feel that behaviourist teaching is a rather dated way of giving information. In the case study, as in most learning situations, you have probably noted that Bob needs to ensure that the students have a grasp of the basic systems and procedures of editing. There are several ways of achieving this, but as you will have found in your own practice, there are time constraints imposed on learning. This may force us to use more directive methods than we would perhaps like in order to ensure that all students are able to perform the actions. This might be achieved through behaviourism. One form of behaviourism that you might be familiar with is Pavlov's idea of classical conditioning (remember the dog, the bell and the food?) but this is a very limited form of learning. If Bob used classical conditioning his students would learn a system or process and be able to repeat it, but they might not be able to transfer the learning to another context (also they very quickly get bored doing the same thing!). Rather than using classical conditioning you may have suggested that Bob uses an alternative behaviouristic approach, possibly that of Skinner or Thorndike. They suggest that you can break tasks into sequential 'chunks' and *reward* learning at each step with constructive feedback. This will give your students a sense of achievement and motivate them to continue learning. All of the students in the case study will need to be motivated to *perform* the processes, which is where behaviourist teaching might be useful, but they will also need to *understand* the processes, which moves us forward to the next school of thought.

Cognitivism/constructivism

The key points of cognitivism are:

* learning is the process of acquiring and storing knowledge in the brain – a bit like a computer;

* learning is a structured process – teachers structure the information for the student by breaking it into small, sequential 'chunks';

* the student builds new knowledge on existing knowledge or previous experience.

The key points of constructivism are:

* students actively participate in learning by organising information so that it is connected to their personal experience or knowledge;

* learning can be a social activity – students learn through discussion with others;

* students 'make meaning' from the learning by applying it to problem solving;

* the role of the teacher is to facilitate learning.

[I]nstead of acquiring habits, learners ... [need to] ... acquire plans and strategies (Hartley, 1998, p 18) so that they can use them as a platform for further learning. You may know that cognitivism is concerned with the physical aspects of learning, looking at the mind and memory, and on the processing and storage/retrieval of information. Learning is progressive, with new learning being added to previous learning, and old, outdated or superseded learning discarded. Teachers can help to link or 'chain' (Gagne, 1985) learning together in the mind of the student by organising the information into sections that build on each other. You may feel that James, who doesn't like the 'theory' element of the course, would benefit from this approach as the teacher can help him to 'chain' theory to the systems and procedures he has learned by showing and explaining to him the connections between the theory and practice of editing. You might also have suggested that Sarah, who lacks confidence when confronted with unfamiliar information or situations, would benefit from the application of Ausubel's (1963) theory of cognitivism. He recommends the use of advance organisers (telling students what, why and how learning is going to happen in advance of the teaching). I'm sure that you will have found when working with students who lack confidence, giving them a sense of the direction the lesson will take removes uncertainty and helps them to prepare themselves to absorb new material more effectively as there are 'no nasty surprises'.

You may find that cognitivism is a useful model in teaching as information is transmitted uniformly, effectively and efficiently. But the student is being taught rather than actively engaging in learning and you will probably have found that this method does not stimulate students' interest for any length of time. Constructivism builds on this theory but moves the emphasis from teaching to learning. Through active participation, students are able to organise the information in a way which is meaningful to them. To facilitate this process Bruner (1960) suggests that teachers use a spiral curriculum, where central concepts are frequently repeated, but with a new layer of information added each time. In your notes you may have suggested that Qasir, who doesn't like repeating things and gets bored quickly, may well benefit from a spiral curriculum approach. Although he is repeating information or concepts, he is still learning new information which will retain his attention.

A (fairly major!) subset of constructivist theory is that of social constructivism which suggests that working with others helps people to learn. Social interaction in the form of discussions or activities with peers or teachers, where ideas can be discussed or plans made together, can help your students as they travel through the zone of proximal development (Vygotsky, 1978) (the journey from what they already know to that which they need to know). Again you may think that all the 'labelled' students would benefit from social learning as a method of learning, particularly if roles are given to them, which allow them to use their talents to help the team. It would suit Qasir's talents to be the facilitator, explaining things to other students in the group. This would ensure that he was engaged in learning and that he was following a spiral curriculum by repeating and adding knowledge or skills to the same topic. Sarah might also benefit as she would be able to use her design skills to help the group while being supported by them in her learning.

Humanism

The key points of humanism are:

* learning is student-centred and personalised – the student is able to make active choices about the learning;

* the student is intrinsically motivated – they want to learn;

* the student helps to construct and guide their learning;

* the teacher's role is that of a facilitator.

Although Qasir might be engaged by the constructivist approach to learning, you may feel that he should be challenged to work on his own towards goals that stretch him. Another school of thought which you might want to think about if you are working with students like Qasir is humanism. This school emphasises person-centred learning in which students have some control over the direction and method of learning. Students develop their own understanding of subjects through research and problem solving, often through working collaboratively with other students. The role of the teacher is to facilitate learning by providing guidance and challenge, and by making students feel valued.

This is an advanced way of learning and you may feel that it is not appropriate to the students in Bob's group at the moment. However, some elements of humanism could be introduced in the latter stages of the project where decisions have to be negotiated in order to fulfil the brief. Although this approach might suit Qasir, it would need to be carefully monitored by the teacher to ensure that all students remain included and engaged in learning.

Critical thinking exercise: differentiating for accessibility

Bob wants to ensure that all the students are able to meet the criteria for the module, particularly the 'labelled' students.

» *What sort of activities do you think he could use to include them in the learning process?*

Differentiation for inclusive classroom practice

Differentiation, like inclusion, is a word that has different meanings for different people and, as you are aware, it is one of the current buzz words in education. It is generally defined along the lines of teachers responding to individual needs (or more prosaically as 'teaching to each') and planning to meet different learning needs in a single lesson. No pressure there then!

As teachers Thomlinson and Allan (2000) suggest, we need to differentiate in three main areas to meet our students' needs:

* their readiness to learn (their entry point into the subject and what they already know);

* their interest (the affinity or curiosity they have for a particular topic or skill); and

* their learning profile (how they learn, their learning styles, their ability level and cognitive skills, and their ability/desire to work co-operatively or independently).

When you read the case study you will have noticed that all of the students have the same type and level of qualification in media, but this does not necessarily mean that their readiness to learn is the same. All three students have an interest in media studies, but again this does not mean that they are all interested in the same aspects of this wide-ranging discipline. They also have very different ways of assimilating information. Sarah, for example, is good at art and this may indicate a preference for visual learning, whereas James likes the tactile elements of media, which might suggest that he learns more effectively kinaesthetically. Qasir? Well, he seems to be bright but …

As I'm sure you will agree our common objective as teachers is to maximise student growth and individual success. In order to do this we need to be able to differentiate in four areas:

* the content of the learning;

* the process of the learning;

* the product of learning;

* the learning environment itself.

Content differentiation

Subject content needs to be differentiated in order to allow all students to access the same curriculum or lesson, so you will need to think about different entry points, learning tasks, and tailoring outcomes to meet your students' needs. In the case study you will have read that Qasir has a good theoretical understanding of editing but little practical expertise; James has the practical skills required but lacks knowledge of the principles of editing; Sarah lacks both knowledge and expertise but has a good eye for art and design and may be able to use this to access the editing module at an intuitive level. All of the students have different entry points and expertise, so a project that includes research, practical application and creativity is needed to enable them to access the module.

Process differentiation

The process of learning – how your students make sense of the facts, concepts and skills of a subject – also needs to be differentiated to enable them to absorb the information. To meet your differentiated learning outcomes you will need to develop activities that can be differentiated according to the interests and prior knowledge of your students as well as the support that they might need. Thinking about the case study as an example of this, Qasir may need a project that will encourage him to use his knowledge of editing theory to create practical demonstrations of different techniques. James could work as part of a group to research editing theory, whereas Sarah could compare and contrast examples of 'before and after' editing. All of these activities are focused on the lesson aim, but the challenge has been changed to reflect the students' differing entry points, their learning styles and the level of support likely to be needed from the teacher.

Product differentiation

As all teachers know, the importance of planning feedback as part of the overall teaching strategy cannot be over-emphasised. Hattie and Timperley (2007) suggest that feedback is one of the most powerful influences on learning and achievement, guiding students through the process of correction and facilitating development. Product is really another description of the type of assessment of learning that can be used to test students' understanding or knowledge. Qasir could be asked to present his project to the class showing practical examples of different types of editing and James could be asked to identify different theorists and develop a handout for the class. Sarah, who Bob knows may not want to speak in front of the class, could be asked to select some examples of before and after editing clips that demonstrate editing techniques in practice which could be prepared as a slide show or video in advance, with her commentary pre-recorded and added to it.

Environmental differentiation

The final piece in the jigsaw is often the one we have least control over. As much as we would like to exercise control over the learning environment, it is frequently determined by the availability of rooms and resources in the specific institution. However, you can alter the layout of most rooms to facilitate group work and establish quiet areas for individual study or project work by providing equipment such as headsets to mitigate sound from computers which might be part of the editing process.

Strategies not a stratagem

As you have seen while working through the case studies, differentiation is not a single strategy that can be applied in your teaching but a series of connected strategies which take into account the subject, its delivery and assessment, to help your students to learn. With thought and planning you can tailor these elements to suit individual students' preferences by engaging them in the process of learning and challenging them at a level appropriate to their skills to support them on their learning journey.

Conclusion

Labels that are positive are likely to have a beneficial effect on both learning and students. However, negative labels are likely to be detrimental to both. Teachers are human beings and all human beings respond to labels in some way and use them to form judgements about students (although they may do this unconsciously) and those judgements can affect the way that we work with our students. As teachers we need to be aware of the potential impact of labelling on teaching and learning, and where possible ensure that all of our students succeed in overcoming and ignoring any negative labels that may be attached to them. By using differentiated teaching techniques in the classroom you will enable all students to access the learning process and attain a measure of success.

Oh and by the way – I still can't do puzzles, but it doesn't bother me now. I've managed to lose my self-imposed label. I have come to realise that not being able to do puzzles is just part of being me, so I head for the e-reader now instead of worrying about it!

Chapter reflections

»   *Labels can have a lasting impact on the 'wearer'.*

»   *If a label is internalised it may become a 'master label' and the wearer will act in accordance with the expectations implied by the label.*

»   *Labels encourage prejudgement of individuals.*

»   *Both teachers and students may align their expectations to the label.*

»   *Using a wide range of approaches can ensure that 'labelled' students can access learning and be included in the learning process.*

Taking it further

National Center on Accessible Instructional Materials, http://aim.cast.org/

A useful site with some excellent links to further reading on both universal design for learning theory and differentiated learning.

Tusting, K and Barton, D (2003) *Models of Adult Learning: A Literature Review.* London: Niace.

An excellent review of major theories and theorists from a range of disciplines whose work informs classroom practice.

References

Ausubel, D (1963) *The Psychology of Meaningful Verbal Learning*. New York: Grune & Stratton.

Becker, H and Howard, S (1963) *Outsiders: Studies in the Sociology of Deviance*. New York: Free Press.

Bloom, B S (1956) *Taxonomy of Educational Objectives, Handbook 1*. New York: David McKay Co. Inc.

Bruner, J (1960) *The Process of Education*. Cambridge, Mass.: Harvard University Press.

Bruner, J (1999) *The Process of Education*. Cambridge, MA.: Harvard University Press.

Department of Children, Schools and Families (2007) *Effective Provision for Gifted and Talented Students in Secondary Education*. Nottingham: DCSF Publications.

Gagné, R M (1985) *The Conditions of Learning*. New York: Holt, Rinehart and Winston.

Goffman, E (1963) *Stigma: Notes on the Management of Spoiled Identity*. Englewood Cliffs, N.J.: Prentice-Hall.

Goodhew, G (2009) *Meeting the Needs of Gifted and Talented Students*. London: Continuum International Publishing Group.

Hartley, J (1998) *Learning and Studying: A Research Perspective*. London: Routledge.

Hattie, J and Timperley, H (2007) The Power of Feedback. *Review of Educational Research*, 77(1, March): 81–112.

Knowles, G (2010) *Supporting Inclusive Practice*. Abingdon: Taylor and Francis.

Lemert, E (1972) *Human Deviance, Social Problems, and Social Control*. Englewood Cliffs, NJ: Prentice Hall.

Reece, I and Walker, S (2007) *Teaching Training and Learning: A Practical Guide*. Sunderland: Business Education Publishers.

Rist, R C (1977) On Understanding the Processes of Schooling: The Contributions of Labeling Theory, in Sadovnik, A, Cookson, P and Semel, S (2001) *Exploring Education* 2nd edn. Boston, MA: Allyn & Bacon, pp 149–57.

Smith, Chris (2005) *Including the Gifted and Talented: Making Inclusion Work for More Gifted and Able Learners*. Abingdon: Taylor & Francis.

Tannenbaum, F (1938) *Crime and the Community*. New York: Columbia University Press.

Tomlinson, C and Allan, S (2000) *Leadership for Differentiating Schools and Classrooms*. Alexandria, VA: ASCD.

Tusting, K and Barton, D (2003) *Models of Adult Learning: A Literature Review*. London: Niace.

Vygotsky, L S(1978) *Mind in Society: The Development of Higher Psychological Processes*. Cambridge, MA: Harvard University Press.

Websites

Betts (sd) *Autonomous Learner Model*. Available at http://nmgifted.org/uploads/2/8/2/3/2823338/autonomous_learner_model.pdf.

Clemson (sd) *Bloom's Taxonomy Action Verbs*. Available at www.clemson.edu/assessment/assessment-practices/referencematerials/documents/Blooms%20Taxonomy%20Action%20Verbs.pdf.

7   NEETs and knots

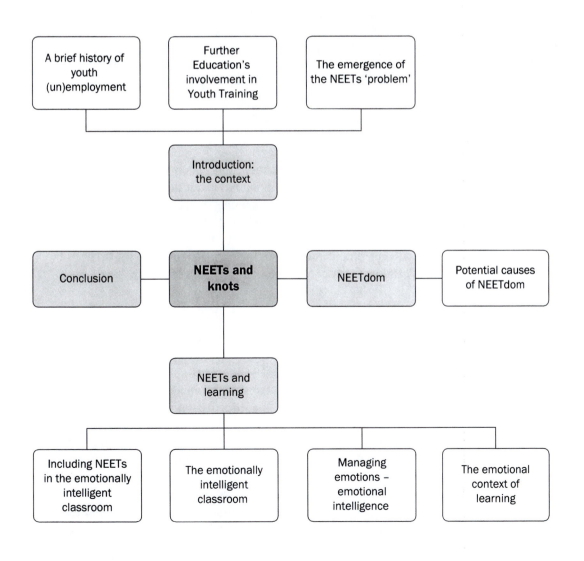

Chapter aims

Although NEETs (Not in Employment Education or Training) is a relatively new category, the problem of youth unemployment regrettably is not. As more and more young people who fall into this category are now entering FE it is important that we as teachers understand their needs and are able to work with them to help them overcome the challenges that they face. The purpose of this chapter is to give you some information on the background of Youth Training, the types of difficulties that cause 'NEETdom', and how to work with NEET students in an emotionally intelligent way.

Introduction: the context

Youth unemployment has been one of the most consistent and worrying trends in unemployment statistics since the late 1960s. Once confined to identifiable problem areas within the UK, youth unemployment, accompanied by a corresponding rise in what are now labelled as NEETs, has reached record levels. Once again concerns are being raised about a 'lost generation' of young people who are at risk of long-term unemployment as they are unable to enter the workforce or sustain employment. The devastating effects of unemployment on young people are clearly documented in the *Youth Index 2014* which notes that *40 per cent of jobless young people say they have faced symptoms of mental illness – including suicidal thoughts, feelings of self-loathing and panic attacks – as a direct result of unemployment* (Prince's Trust, 2014, p 3). One route that has clearly been identified by successive governments as a remedy for youth unemployment has been that of continued education or training. Since the late 1960s consecutive administrations have introduced expensive initiatives focused on education or training, but none have successfully, or in a sustained way, addressed the problem. The role that the FE sector has had to play in these initiatives has been variously foregrounded or ignored by government policy. However, the two elements at the centre of the acronym NEET – 'education' and 'employment' – are also those that lie at the heart of the FE sector, and its response to the problem of NEETs forms the focus of this chapter.

A brief history of youth (un)employment

The 1940s and 1950s

Two main factors have shaped youth employment in the post-war years: the political and social philosophies of the government and the changing demands of the economy. In the period immediately after the Second World War the Education Act (1944) was introduced as part of the welfare state legislation. Part-time education or training was made available for anyone at work who was not already receiving training under the apprenticeship system. However, with demand for labour outstripping supply, high wages and easy access to unskilled or semi-skilled work, few young people took up the offer of free post-compulsory education. Youth employment levels remained reasonably buoyant throughout the 1950s, but in the 1960s overseas competition challenged the manufacturing sector and the introduction of new, less labour-intensive technologies changed the type of labour required.

The 1960s and 1970s

Gradually the economic situation worsened and youth unemployment levels rose to a level where the government had to step in. Youth unemployment was for the first time recognised as a national rather than a local problem. The Manpower Services Commission (MSC), the Employment Service Agency and the Training Services Agency were established, and in 1975 a Job Creation Programme was set up to create 15,000 temporary jobs for young people. Government subsidies were made available for employers who recruited school leavers, with higher levels of subsidy being made available in the following year for employers who recruited young people under 20 who had been unemployed for more than six months. By the late 1970s the principle that unemployed school leavers should have access to government-funded training schemes was firmly established.

The 1980s and 1990s

In 1981 one in three school leavers was entering the Youth Opportunities Programme which was run by FE colleges and private training providers. The twin approach of employer subsidies and training schemes was continued throughout the 1980s with the launch of a one-year Youth Training Scheme (YTS) in 1983 which was extended to two years in 1986. Youth unemployment, however, remained stubbornly high, and in 1989 the YTS was replaced by Youth Training (YT) and it became impossible for young people to obtain unemployment benefit if they were not registered into YT, where they received a training allowance.

Further Education's involvement in Youth Training

As can be seen from the subtle changes in the title of the schemes, as the youth unemployment figures rose there was an increased emphasis on training rather than employment in government schemes. The training element was formalised with the introduction of National Vocational Qualifications (NVQs) in 1986 which were designed to provide and accredit work-based skills. These qualifications were quickly adopted by FE which was more able to deal with the rapid changes in funding that led to the closure of many of the private training providers, and far better equipped to implement and deliver formal qualifications. Further changes which emphasised the importance of the training and education for employment elements of the schemes were introduced in the 1990s. 'Quality training' in the form of Modern Apprenticeships (MAs) was introduced and forged a partnership between the employers who provided the work experience for students and FE which provided access to qualifications.

The emergence of the NEETs 'problem'

Many FE teachers, and this may include you, have seen significant changes in the MAs over the past few years (including the recent change which incorporates GCSE English and mathematics into the framework). But the MA system remains the model pathway for those who wish to leave school and are able to gain employment with training. However, there remains the significant problem of those who are unable, unwilling or unready to access the labour, training or Further Education markets – the NEETs of the title. From 2003, this group were offered an access programme called Entry to Employment (E2E) consisting of three major strands: basic skills, personal and social development, and accredited vocational training.

The programme was intended to be sufficiently adaptable to enable it to be conducted in a variety of settings (FE colleges, Prince's Trust, youth centres, etc.) in order to maximise its potential to re-engage disaffected young people and to meet their individual needs.

Critical thinking activity: what is a NEET?

Think about young people who may be classified as NEETs and try to answer the questions below. You may have taught some students who are classified as NEETs and you could use them as a starting point for this activity.

» *What characteristics do you think NEETs share?*

» *What are their barriers to learning?*

NEETdom

Potential causes of NEETdom

Overall, NEETs get a pretty bad press. Spours and Stone in their preface to the findings in the 2009 LSN report on NEETs state that:

> *The range of issues associated with young people in the NEET category comprises low educational attainment, homelessness, gang membership, early criminalisation, drug culture and dependency, care needs, teenage pregnancy, prostitution and, in many or even most cases, multiple and overlapping disadvantage, for example, pregnancy, drug dependency and crime.*
>
> (LSN, 2009, p 7)

Phew! Quite a list! There is no doubt that many NEETs do, as Leadbeater (2008) notes, lead complicated lives with lower levels of income and poorer life chances than others in the same age group. But you may also find that the range of difficulties causing young people to join the ranks of the NEETs can be as simple (although no less problematic for those affected) as inadequate public transport in rural areas, which can seriously impact on their ability to take up an offer of employment, education or training. You may also find that most young people who fall into the NEETs category have left school with few formal qualifications. NEETs often also lack the social and interpersonal skills, confidence, self-esteem and motivation they need to gain and retain employment, and may not have the social networks and family links that can help them gain a foothold in the workforce.

All too frequently those in the NEETs category are portrayed by the media as a group of feckless ne'er do wells with little ambition or motivation. However, those of you who work or plan to work with NEETs in FE will generally find that their ambitions are pretty *similar to those of other young people (albeit that their expectations of achieving these aspirations were lower)* (LSN, 2009, p 1). Most of them want to gain employment and be able to participate in society rather than being part of a marginalised minority. The trouble is that many NEETs don't see education as a way of acquiring the skills to gain employment. They have been 'turned off' learning by an education system which, for them, represents a source of failure. The LSN

Report (2009) suggests that this sense of failure is not caused by any problems they had with the curriculum but by difficult interpersonal relationships within the school environment and their interactions with the authority structure of the school. These potential causes of disaffection are explored by Duffy and Elwood (2013) whose research suggests that the young people's difficulties fall into four main categories: their relationship with the teacher; their response to the label of being poor or disaffected students; the quality of their relationship with their peers; and the quality of teaching in terms of the range of approaches used by teachers. These findings would seem to indicate the importance of the emotional response of students to learning. It is possible that emotional alienation rather than a lack of intellectual ability or unwillingness to engage with subject matter is responsible (at least in part) for young people becoming NEETs.

NEETs and learning

The emotional context of learning

All of your students are in a process of development. This is particularly true of the young adults in FE who are coping with the strain of making the transition from childhood to adulthood on social, physical, psychological and emotional levels simultaneously, a process which may be exhibited in the general moodiness that many parents (and possibly you as their teacher!) sometimes feel characterise young people in their teenage years. The 'normal' students in your classes, those with stable home backgrounds and expected patterns of development, generally deal with these transitions reasonably well. But those of your students with more problematic personal, social or emotional circumstances, such as NEETs students, find these changes more challenging and stressful to deal with and their difficulties may generate extreme emotional outbursts in response to seemingly trivial triggers.

Emotional responses

Buckler and Castle (2014, following Niendenthal et al., 2006) note that there are six basic emotions which fall into two categories; anger or rage, fear and sadness (or dejection) are negative emotions, while surprise, excitement and joy are positive emotions. Other emotions can be added to this list and one of the best-known models is that of Plutchik's (1980) emotional wheel which contains eight emotional elements divided into two groups of polar opposites:

joy	sadness
trust (acceptance)	disgust
fear	anger
surprise	anticipation

These emotions are frequently combined to produce further emotions, for example:

- anticipation + joy = optimism;
- joy + trust = love;
- trust (acceptance) + fear = submission;
- fear + surprise = awe;
- surprise + sadness = disapproval;
- sadness + disgust = remorse;
- disgust + anger = contempt;
- anger + anticipation = aggression.

Our emotional response to any situation is governed by the most primitive part of the brain, the limbic system. This controls many of our basic emotions and motivations, particularly those that are related to our basic instincts, such as fear and anger, or more enjoyable emotions such as the pleasure gained from eating. As primitive reactions that were originally intended to help us survive, they form the immediate, uncontrolled, knee-jerk responses of individuals to situations which we find threatening. They jump into action before the neo-cortex (the rational part of the brain) can exercise its calming logical influence. As adults we have learned to govern our emotions, to think before we act; but our students' emotions are not necessarily always under their control and this can lead to what you as a teacher might see as an irrational response to a situation. Our emotions are generated by a need to react instantaneously, but their effect can be more lasting, and an intense emotional experience can affect the mood of an individual for a period of time, and in that time frame it can impact on the individual's general outlook on life and sense of well-being.

Managing emotions – emotional intelligence

The management of emotional responses is generally defined as emotional intelligence (EI), a term coined by Salovey and Mayer (1990, p 189). EI is the cognitive processes that allow us to both recognise and control our own feelings and emotions; to understand those of other people; and to use this information as a guide for taking action. Goleman (1996) later changed EI to include the social as well as the psychological aspects of emotional responsiveness. For Goleman, EI consists of a number of interrelated elements:

- self-awareness – the understanding of personal emotions and their impact on others;
- self-regulation – the ability to control emotions and to think before acting;
- internal motivation – the desire to achieve;
- empathy – the understanding of others and an ability to respond to the emotional state of others;
- social skills – the management of relationships and building of networks by developing a rapport with individuals and groups.

The inability to control or to understand these factors can have an impact on the behaviour of individuals and their sense of inclusion in FE. You may find that many of the NEETs students you come into contact with in FE have failed in education and sometimes in society due to their inability to control some or all of the factors which Goleman argues form EI. However, you should remember that while most young people will acquire a level of EI as part of the normal pattern of growth and development, there are also individuals on the autistic spectrum who are unable to gain a full understanding of these elements.

CASE STUDY

Kyle's story

Well, one day I just told her to stick her stupid essay didn't I? What's the point in knowing that stuff anyway? It's not going to be any good to me. It's just stupid learning about dead people isn't it, there's just no point in it. 'Go and look it up on your own' she said. Look what up? What was I supposed to be looking up? And then she looked at me as though I was thick when I said I couldn't do it. I kept on telling her I couldn't do it and I didn't know what to do but she told me I was rude and threw me out of the lesson, so I was in trouble with the Head again. She always picked on me because I didn't like her stupid subject – it's just so boring, all that copying and writing and stuff. I hate reading and writing; and I hate her. She is always mean to me and she only wants to teach the ones who are going to get good grades anyway. I mean what is the point? How is it going to help me get a job as a mechanic? I want to do things not write boring things down. I know I shouldn't have done it; it's got me into loads more trouble with the school again. School just sucks!

The teacher's story

Well he just flipped again didn't he? All you have to do is say no to that boy or just look at him in the wrong way and he goes for it, shouting, being rude and swearing. He says he doesn't know what he is supposed to do but he has been told what to do, exactly the same as all the others, and most of them just get on with their work. I know he isn't the world's most academic student but he just doesn't try. He just sits there and draws most of the time, no eye contact or anything. The other students don't want to work with him as he doesn't contribute in group work, just makes silly suggestions and disrupts them, but when he's asked to do something on his own he just flips. Difficult boy! Heading for the dole queue that one.

Critical thinking activity

» *What do you think are the main causes of Kyle's discontent?*

» *How has the learning situation affected Kyle's behaviour and learning?*

Learning as an holistic experience

As you will have gathered, Kyle has very strong feelings about this particular learning experience! You will have noted that in a whole-class teaching situation he felt disengaged from a subject that he saw as irrelevant to his future needs and a task which he felt he could not achieve. Although learning is an individual process, students also experience learning situations holistically so that in addition to the cognitive and physical aspects of learning which Kyle was struggling with you may have suggested that he was also experiencing difficulty in the *attitudinal, emotive, evaluative … and sense… dimension* (Jarvis et al., 2004, p 60). In fact he was not coping with learning in any of the three domains. In teacher education programmes you will have learned about the importance of the three domains of knowledge: cognitive (to do with thinking and understanding), affective (to do with attitudes, emotions and feelings) and psychomotor (to do with physical co-ordination, dexterity and skill) (*Bloom's Taxonomy*, 1956). In FE all teachers (and I'm sure you're no exception to this) are under pressure to make sure that their students achieve measurable goals or outcomes (qualifications and examinations). In many instances the most effective way for busy teachers like you to achieve these results is to concentrate on the cognitive and psychomotor aspect when planning lesson outcomes or objectives and developing learning activities. Unfortunately the emotional impact of the lesson on the student (and their learning) is not always given the same level of consideration.

Kyle was upset by the 'attitude' of the teacher and you will have noted that he feels that he is treated differently to his peers. He also feels that the teacher has a low opinion of his academic ability and favours those she identifies as 'good' students who are more able than he is and who are likely to achieve good grades in the subject. His fixed ideas about the learning situation, combined with his immediate concerns about his lack of understanding of the assignment and fear of failure, caused him to become angry and aggressive towards the teacher and eventually in him telling her to *stick her stupid essay*. When reading through the case study you will have seen that at the end of his comments Kyle knew that his outburst was neither rational nor acceptable and there is even a hint of remorse for his actions in his final remarks. All your students will find it difficult to control their emotions at times, particularly when they are in situations that they find threatening or which remind them of negative experiences. Some of your students who have low emotional flashpoints and poor self-management skills are likely to respond negatively to classroom situations they find stressful and this may result in 'bad' behaviour. For some, particularly those who have negative previous experiences of education which make them feel threatened or insecure (like many NEETs students that you will meet in FE), this emotional response becomes a habit that they find difficult to break and they need help from emotionally intelligent teachers to learn to manage their emotions.

Critical thinking activity

The case study above clearly shows that Kyle struggles to control his emotions at times.

»   *How do you think it could be made easier for him to control his reactions in the classroom situation?*

The emotionally intelligent classroom

As we saw in the last section, the affective domain of learning frequently receives less attention than the cognitive and psychomotor domains. As a teacher you will undoubtedly try to use SMART (specific, measurable, achievable, realistic and timebound) differentiated lesson outcomes, but you may already have found that it is difficult to set SMART objectives for learning in the affective domain. This is in part due to the difficulty of showing how you are going to work in the affective domain in the lesson – after all, unlike the other two domains, it is dealing with something that does not necessarily lead to an immediate, tangible, measurable outcome. Although it may not appear as a specific outcome on a lesson plan, expertise in this domain is often an important part of the 'hidden curriculum', and knowing how to use the affective domain in teaching is an essential part of your 'toolkit'. By understanding how to work in the affective domain you will be able to create an emotionally intelligent classroom and give your students a pleasurable, holistic and inclusive experience of learning.

The effect of poor relationship management

In the first critical thinking activity in this chapter you identified areas that might characterise a NEET student. Although the range of characteristics you may have identified is wide, many NEETs students have for one reason or another failed to engage with education. Like Kyle in the case study above, some of them may feel that educational establishments are unsafe or even threatening environments (despite their outward displays of bravado and streetwise attitudes). Earlier in the chapter you read Duffy and Elwood's (2013) claim that two of the primary causes of 'NEEThood' are the quality of relationships with peers and with teachers. The causes of the difficulties that NEETs students experience in these areas are many and varied and could be psychological, physiological, emotional and social in origin. As a result of these difficulties you may find that many young NEET students need help in order to establish and maintain positive relationships with their peers and teachers before they can be re-engaged in education.

NEET students are generally very aware that they are in a position of relative powerlessness in relation to teachers; something that can be made worse when they feel 'disrespected' by teachers who they feel regard them as children rather than as young adults and individuals. A student's feeling of powerlessness can easily turn into a feeling of helplessness if they find themselves working with peers who appear more competent than they are, or on tasks that they feel are irrelevant or beyond their capabilities. These feelings of powerlessness and helplessness add fuel to their existing sense of a lack of personal control and self-esteem. This negative spiral of emotions may eventually lead to the withdrawal of effort – just giving up – or in an outburst of 'unacceptable behaviour' in order to deflect further damage away from their already fragile self-image.

Promoting emotional development

Cox (2000 in Topping and Maloney, 2005, p 65) suggests that the actions of teachers, their *behaviour and attitudes towards their pupils, their expectations regarding them ... have a powerful influence upon ... academic motivation and progress* of vulnerable students such as NEETs. All of your students, and particularly NEET students, appreciate interesting lessons linked to real life; rules that are fair but enforced consistently; helpful (but not patronising) explanations of difficult areas; and teachers who are approachable and respectful. As we have seen earlier, many NEETs students experience difficulty in dealing with situations or relationships in which they feel they have little control. Working with them to develop their sense of control and empowering them to take increasing levels of responsibility and autonomy in learning is challenging – but possible – and very rewarding.

You will probably have come across Maslow's Hierarchy of Needs (1954) in which he identifies a number of basic needs for individual growth. When his theory is applied to teaching and learning you will see that the need for social and emotional stability and self-esteem are critical steps in a student's personal development. Rogers (1961) built on the work of Maslow and suggested that in order for an individual to develop their sense of 'self-worth' (self-esteem) they need to know that other people view them positively. For Rogers there are three important elements in developing an individual's self-worth:

•   they need a nurturing and inclusive environment that provides them with 'genuineness' (openness and honesty from other people);

•   acceptance or unconditional positive regard (being accepted by others for who and what they are); and

•   empathy (being listened to and their views and concerns understood by others).

In the FE environment your role as a teacher in developing these elements is crucial as you are the one who can create the emotional environment for learning which NEET students will perceive as inclusive. Having read this, please don't go away with the idea that when working with NEETs students you should become a social worker rather than a teacher. If you are working with NEETs there will undoubtedly be a need for an increased emphasis in meeting the emotional as well as the academic needs of the student. However, although you may need to call upon your reserves of empathy, your primary role remains that of a teacher but one who creates, and works within, a consciously inclusive learning environment.

An inclusive and emotionally intelligent learning environment can help create the conditions for learning. But, as Bruner (1966) notes, in addition students must be ready to learn and the subject must be presented in a way that the student can understand. One way of doing this, he suggests (and you may well do it already), is to design learning so that the student is able to make connections with their previous experience. Looking back at Kyle in the case study it would seem that none of these conditions are met, and in Bruner's terms Kyle lacked the necessary *state of readiness* to learn – in Kyle's terms his situation *just sucked*.

Including NEETs in the emotionally intelligent classroom

As a teacher you know that most students *learn* through visual, kinaesthetic and interpersonal techniques, but as teachers we often rely heavily on verbal techniques to *teach*. The work of Gardner (1983) and Sternberg (1985) challenged this way of teaching and encouraged multi-modal teaching, which uses active student participation to include students in the learning process. 'Old hat' some of you might be saying; but look at your own practice and just think how much of your time you spend talking to your students – it's probably more than you thought! Gardner thought that people learned in different ways and initially identified seven forms of intelligence: linguistic, mathematical, visual-spatial, kinaesthetic, musical, interpersonal and intrapersonal. By appealing to different senses and abilities you know from your own practice that students feel more included in learning and learn more effectively. As we saw in Chapter 3, the term *intelligence* used in this sense can be distracting and you can substitute the word *competence* if it makes you feel more comfortable with the idea.

Although the idea of learning styles and different forms of intelligence are contentious and have been the subject of much debate in education, both ideas can be very useful when developing an emotionally intelligent classroom. Many of the NEETs that you will meet in FE think, like Kyle in the case study, that learning is all about writing boring things down. You may find that working with the wide-ranging, interactive, differentiated and inclusive teaching methods that appeal to different intelligences can also help you to challenge and motivate your students. Sternberg (1985) felt that students needed to be challenged on three levels: the analytical (problem solving and evaluation), practical (ideas and understanding relevant to everyday life) and creative (formulation of new ideas). If you as a teacher can offer NEET students the prospect of learning in ways that avoid the methods which have proved so problematic for them in the past (not all the time but at least some of it) then you can begin to break down their barriers to learning and develop their 'readiness to learn'. Some of the different ways of learning suggested in Multiple Intelligence Theory can help you to achieve this.

Using emotional intelligence to affect behaviour

Bostock and Wood (2012) suggest that inclusive learning should be an active, creative, focused, busy, interactive and challenging way of learning, which means that your classroom might at times be messy, loud, competitive and humorous. The responsibility for developing this type of learning, although it remains with you as the teacher, can also be shared with your NEET students. For example, one of the primary aims of NEET education programmes is to help them learn socially acceptable behaviours. But as we have seen with Kyle, NEETs students are very aware of their status both as young adults who demand *respect* and of being perceived as *bad* students, who become disaffected and disengaged from learning because of their experiences of the education system.

A first step in learning new patterns of behaviour is for them to understand why they need to change. This is unlikely to happen if they feel they are in a threatening environment where they are likely to default to a negative emotional response. As a teacher you need to find ways of making them feel secure so that they can learn to break the emotional cycle and think about their responses rather than react negatively out of habit. One way of doing this is to enable your students to 'own' the learning context by involving them in negotiating the rules by which it will be governed. By including NEET students in an adult way you are not only empowering them by respecting their views, but you are also modelling the rational and logical patterns of behaviour that you want to encourage. You can build on this initial empowerment by encouraging your students to participate in designing their learning for parts of the programme, although this may not be possible where a qualification route is being followed. However, you can include your students in the delivery of the programme by discussing the reasons for particular types of input; exploring the reasons for activities; looking at what they can expect to learn from participating; showing how the subject fits in with their current experience and how it links to their future lives and learning.

Initially your NEET students may find group work and discussions challenging as they may be more used to opting out of group work rather than actively participating. But by organising short, timed, focused activities with discrete, positive outcomes carried out in engineered groups you can promote peer interaction. You may however find that you have to renegotiate ground rules on participation, communication and turn-taking with NEET students in order for group work to be effective. You may also need to discreetely monitor groups to make sure that the rules are enforced appropriately, offering firm and consistent praise of developing interpersonal skills rather than singling out or criticising those whose EI skills are less established.

Your students will appreciate being challenged, but it is essential that you differentiate activities and resources to ensure that all the students are able to access the subject at a level which is appropriate to their skills. One way of doing this is to use a cognitivist approach which ensures that tasks and processes are taught in sequential bite-sized chunks combined with problem-based learning. By carefully building tasks you will help your students to practise generic problem-solving skills, such as clarifying or defining the problem; identifying and evaluating alternative solutions; and reflecting on the choices and processes involved in reaching a conclusion. Using problem solving as part of the learning process will also help your students to gain skills that are found in the affective domain such as assertiveness and empathy; and through discussion and interaction students will be able to see the relevance of these to real-life situations.

Conclusion

Working with emotional intelligence, dealing with the expectations (and fears!) of students, planning the emotional environment and the physical experience of learning are all difficult. The NEETs students that you encounter in FE are often vulnerable emotionally and psychologically (although they may not appear to be on the surface). Having failed to thrive socially, emotionally or academically in compulsory education they are quite naturally resistant to participating further in education and may prefer the negative status of being a NEET to confronting the challenge of change. Re-including them in education is not just a case of offering a different type of course or a different institution. NEETdom needs to be addressed at a more fundamental level, that of beliefs and values. This is not easy, but you may find that helping students in this category to develop their self-belief and re-establish levels of positive self-esteem as part of a wider educational process of 'becoming' (Colley et al., 2003) a fully rounded and included student is one of the most rewarding aspects of your role as a teacher.

Chapter reflections

»   *NEETs, although a relatively new category applied to young people, is linked to the history of initiatives to address youth unemployment.*

»   *The causes of NEEThood are varied and many NEETs face challenging and chaotic personal circumstances which affect learning.*

»   *Emotions precede formal learning, so the student has to feel comfortable and ready to learn before the learning of new material can begin.*

»   *The importance of an emotionally intelligent and stable setting for learning cannot be overestimated in including NEET students in education and/or training.*

Taking it further

Duffy, G. and Elwood, J. (2013) The Perspectives of 'Disengaged' Students in the 14–19 Phase on Motivations and Barriers to Learning within the Context of Institutions and Classrooms. *London Review of Education*, 11(2): 112–26.

A look at education from the point of view of those who are disengaged.

Goleman, D. (1996) *Emotional Intelligence: Why It Can Matter More Than IQ*. New York: Bantam Books.

The seminal work on the theory and importance of emotional intelligence.

References

Bartlett, S and Burton, D (2012) *Introduction to Education Studies*. London: Sage.

Bloom, B S (1956) *Taxonomy of Educational Objectives, Handbook I: The Cognitive Domain*. New York: David McKay Co. Inc.

Bostock, J and Wood, J (2012) *Teaching 14–19 A Handbook*. Maidenhead: Open University Press.

Bruner, J (1966) *Toward a Theory of Instruction*. Cambridge, MA: Harvard University Press.

Buckler, S and Castle, P (2014) *Psychology for Teachers*. London: Sage.

Colley, C, James, D, Tedder, M and Diment, K (2003) Learning as Becoming in Vocational Education and Training: Class, Gender and the Role of Vocational Habitus. *Journal of Vocational Education and Training*, 55(4): 471–96.

Cox, T (2005) Combating Educational Disadvantage: Meeting the Needs of Vulnerable Children, in Topping, K and Maloney, S (eds) *The RoutledgeFalmer Reader in Inclusive Education*. Abingdon: Routledge.

Duffy, G and Elwood, J (2013) The Perspectives of 'Disengaged' Students in the 14–19 Phase on Motivations and Barriers to Learning within the Context of Institutions and Classrooms. *London Review of Education*, 11(2): 112–26.

Gardner, H (1983) *Frames of Mind: The Theory of Multiple Intelligences*. London: Fontana.

Goleman, D (1996) *Emotional Intelligence: Why It Can Matter More Than IQ*. New York: Bantam Books.

Haughey, A (2007) Pupils Disengaged from School: Evaluation of an Alternative Vocational Education Programme. *Education and Child Psychology*, 24(1): 52–55.

Jarvis, M (2005) *The Psychology of Effective Learning and Teaching*. Cheltenham: Nelson Thornes.

Jarvis, P, Holford, J and Griffin, C (2004) *The Theory and Practice of Learning*. London: RoutledgeFalmer.

Kolb, D A (1984) *Experiential Learning Experience as a Source of Learning and Development*. New Jersey: Prentice Hall.

Lawy, R, Quinn, J and Diment, K (2009) Listening to 'The Thick Bunch': (Mis)understanding and (Mis) representation of Young People in Jobs without Training in the South West of England. *British Journal of Sociology of Education*, 30(6): 741–55.

Leadbeater, C (2008) A NEET Solution. *New Statesman*, 14 July, p 16.

Lynch, L. (1994) *Training in the Private Sector: International Comparisons*. London: University of Chicago Press.

Maslow, A H (1954) *Motivation and Personality*. New York: Harper and Row.

Niedenthal, P, Krauth-Gruber, S and Ric, F (2006) *Psychology of Emotion Interpersonal, Experimental, and Cognitive Approaches*. Abingdon: Taylor and Francis.

Plutchik, R (1980) *Emotion, Theory, Research and Experience* Vol. 1: *Theories of Emotion*. New York: Academic.

Rogers, C (1961) *On Becoming a Person*. Boston: Houghton Mifflin.

Sternberg, R (1985) *Beyond IQ: A Triarchic Theory of Intelligence*. Cambridge: Cambridge University Press.

Topping, K and Maloney, S (2005) *The RoutledgeFalmer Reader in Inclusive Education*. Abingdon: Routledge.

Websites

Bell, R and Jones, G (2002) Youth Policies in the UK: A Chronological Map 2nd edn www.keele.ac.uk/depts/so/youthchron/about/printable.htm. Available at www.keele.ac.uk/youthpolicies.

Fleming, N D and Mills, C (1992). Not Another Inventory, Rather a Catalyst for Reflection. To Improve the Academy, 11: 37–49. Available at http://digitalcommons.unl.edu/cgi/viewcontent.cgi?article=1245&context=podimproveacad.

Gagné, R (1965) *Instructional Design, Conditions of Learning*. Available at www.instructionaldesign.org/theories/conditions-learning.html.

LSN (2009) *Tackling the NEETs Problem: Supporting Local Authorities in Reducing Young People not in Employment, Education and Training*. London: LSN. Available at www.ioe.ac.uk/tacklingneets.pdf.

Gartshore, I, Haydn, T and Lane, K (2009) *Neet in West Norfolk: an Enquiry into the Issue of Young People who are not in Education, Employment or Training*. Available at www.uea.ac.uk/~m242/neet/neettestimony.pdf.

Oxford Student Mental Health Network. Available at www.osmhn.org.uk/event/emotional_intelligence_in_teaching_and_learning_-_practical_strategies.

Prince's Trust Macquarie Youth Index 2014, www.princes-trust.org.uk/pdf/YOUTH_INDEX_2014.pdf.

Salovey, P and Mayer, J (1990) Emotional Intelligence. Available at www.unh.edu/emotional_intelligence/EIAssets/EmotionalIntelligenceProper/EI1990%20Emotional%20Intelligence.pdf.

Spielhofer, T, Marson-Smith, H and Evans, K (2009) *Non-formal Learning: Good Practice in Re-engaging Young People who are NEET*. Slough: NFER. Available at www.nfer.ac.uk/nfer/publications/LIN01/LIN01.pdf.

8 Special students

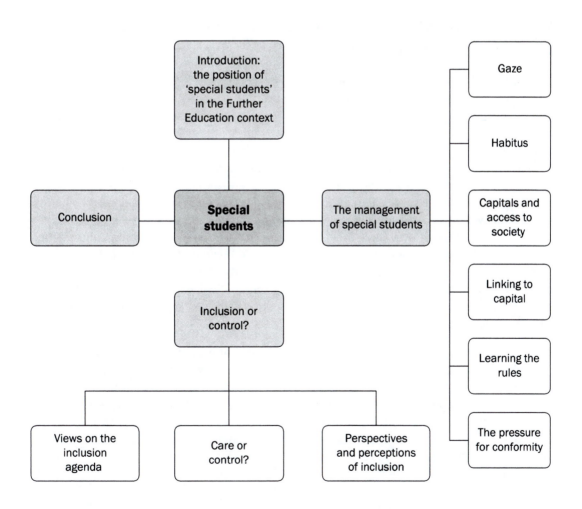

Chapter aims

This chapter will help you to:

- understand the position of special students in FE;

- reflect on competing analyses of the inclusion of special students in education and wider society;

- explore the role of FE in providing special students with access to economic, social and cultural capital;

- reflect on the conflicting roles of FE as an enabler and a controller of special students.

Introduction: the position of 'special students' in the Further Education context

All students are special in their own way; but, to misquote George Orwell, *some students are more special than others*. Anecdotal evidence from FE colleges suggests that the number of students with moderate learning difficulties (MLD) or profound and multiple learning difficulties (PMLD) has risen steadily over the past few years, although accurate statistics on the number of students from these groups participating in FE are scarce. Unlike the animals in Orwell's allegory of society who could be described as a 'special' group because they wielded power and influence over others, the students who are the focus of this chapter may be deemed 'special' for the opposite reason. They are often those who lack status and influence in the society of the FE college. Like Orwell's *Animal Farm*, FE colleges are microcosms of a wider society; although they have their own rules, regulations, norms, values and relationships which influence, mould and shape those individuals who form that society, they are also responsive to external forces and controls. Just as the development of Animal Farm was influenced by the external pressures of the prevailing political, economic and social context, so FE has had to respond to the same types of influences in evolving an inclusive relationship with both MLD and PMLD students.

Allan (1996) notes a number of different perspectives that have been used when discussing special students, some of which have been discussed in other chapters in this book. There are three ways of viewing educational difficulty. The deficit model locates the educational difficulty within the student; the curriculum model suggests that the difficulty lies within the materials and methods of learning whereas the social constructivist model is concerned with the ways in which students and teachers react to the labels assigned to special students. The purpose of this chapter is to examine the different strategies adopted by the FE sector as it responds to external pressures to include these students and to examine the impact that these strategies have had on the institutions, teachers and students themselves. We will be using the analytical tools of influential philosophers Michel Foucault and Pierre Bourdieu to do this. Foucault wrote about minority groups and discrimination, including those who would now be described as having special needs, and also about education. Bourdieu, like Foucault, wrote about education, he did not write about students with special needs directly, but his analytical tools can be used to analyse their position in society and education.

Critical thinking activity: the institution's view

» *Read the following conversation between a tutor teaching mainstream students at an FE college and an adult student taking a part-time vocational course. As you read make some notes on what you feel the passage reveals about the college's attitude towards students with MLD or PMLD.*

CASE STUDY

Student: *Are you sure that there are students at the college who come in wheelchairs and have this profound or multiple learning difficulty thing? I've never seen anyone like that here. You must keep them well hidden.*

Tutor: *Well, not really hidden, but they are taught on the ground floor because it's easier for wheelchair access from the side entrance. It was put in especially for them and the doors down there are all electric and have buttons at the right level so that anyone in a wheelchair, or being pushed in a wheelchair, can open them easily.*

Student: *But are they here at the same time as us? Apart from the young lady in the wheelchair who gets herself around I've never seen anyone who needs that much help. So where do they all go for coffee and dinner breaks then? They don't go in the same café area as us do they?*

Tutor: *Well no. They are here at the same time as you, but because they need a lot of support and some of them have mobility difficulties it's easier for them all to use the refectory area rather than the café, although they can go to the café area if their support staff want to take them there. There are ramps so there is disabled access, but if it is busy there sometimes isn't a lot of space, and remember, you can always go to the refectory if you want to.*

Student: *So are there classrooms there then? I thought it was just college offices.*

Tutor: *Yes, but the classrooms down there are usually used by the MLD and PMLD students. Other staff sometimes can use them if they aren't being used by those groups. Again they're there partly because of the access situation – we need to make sure that all students are safe if there is an emergency like a fire or something, and they can all get out of the building safely from there. The classrooms were also specially designed so that there is extra space for students with mobility issues, and of course we need to make sure that there is enough space to accommodate the support staff who work with them, and any special teaching equipment that the teacher needs.*

Student: *But all the rooms on that floor that I've seen have got keypad entry systems, so have the classrooms got them too?*

Tutor: Well yes. But if you think about it that's mainly for safety reasons isn't it? We want to make sure that the students don't wander off or get lost. The college is a big building when all is said and done. We've also got another block on the site which a lot of them go to for practical activities and that's all set out for them to learn cooking and independence skills.

Student: OK, so they've got access to the building and they've got classrooms and space and resources and things here, and they've got another building that they use, but what do you actually teach them?

Tutor: Well …

The management of special students

Gaze

The term 'gaze' is probably most easily understood if you think about it as being the way in which things are viewed. For example, the way in which FE 'treats', 'manages' or 'works with' special students is determined by the way in which society views (or gazes at) these students at a particular time. As we have seen in earlier chapters, social and political pressures have changed the focus of inclusion in education. Initially groups that were seen as 'different', special needs for example, were ignored by the education system. When society and education became more common the system tried to deal with their difference by segregation, placing special needs students in special schools or institutions. As society changed again (very recently, as this change can be traced back to the Warnock Report of 1978) special needs students were integrated into mainstream FE where they were treated differently from other students as they had help in the classroom in the form of Learning Support Assistants (LSAs) to meet their needs, or were perhaps in special classes where they were taught separately in the mainstream premises. They were accepted as part of FE but still labelled as being different. Finally special needs students are being recognised as being part of FE and FE has adapted to meet their needs so that teachers like you now differentiate your lessons to ensure that all your students are included and additional support is given where needed. Each time society changes its opinion or gaze in relation to special needs students the focus of the education system changes and the way in which special needs students are educated changes.

The particular groups of students which are the focus of this chapter are more challenging for FE than students with special needs who are now part of the mainstream classroom. They are both the *object* of the educational gaze of FE (which identifies them as being in need of specialist support) and its *subject*, as the nature of the educational support that they needed has been identified and is supported by state funding. Their difficulties are more severe and they will have attended special schools and/or received intensive in-class support throughout their education. From the conversation that you have read between the student and the tutor you may feel that these students are included as they are located within the college. However, because they need specialised facilities to meet their specific needs you might think that they are also excluded as they are segregated from other students and use discrete (and discreet) classrooms, separate entrances, etc. in the main building, as well as having a completely separate facility on another part of the site. In Foucault's view then, these students are subject to two different gazes at the same time within FE – the gaze of inclusion and that of exclusion.

Habitus

For Bourdieu, education is a field or an area of society. Each field is part of wider society and is influenced by it, but it is also a separate area. This is not an easy concept to understand but it might help you to think about a farm with lots of fields. Some of them grow crops; others have sheep or cattle on them. In the crops area of the farm several different types of crops are grown, each in a separate field with a fence round it, but they are still all crops. These fields can also be divided down to form sub-fields which don't necessarily have a fence round them but which the farmer recognises as being slightly different and so he treats these areas slightly differently, perhaps adding a bit more fertiliser to them to try to help them fit in with the rest of the field. The farm is society itself, the area of the farm growing crops we will call education. Within the education area are small fields each growing a different crop – or type of education such as FE or compulsory education. Each of these fields is separated by a fence but is still part of the education area of the farm. Each field or type of education has different characteristics. So, for example, compulsory education gives a basic general education to students, while universities give a more specialist subject-focused education. Therefore, in many respects each field has its own separate identity, ways of working and values. Each of these fields can be divided down further into subject specialisms, for example, or areas that work with particular types of students like our special students. And because they have slightly different characteristics they too can have their own slightly different identity, ways of working and values.

This identity, or habitus, structures the way that people in that field see their work. So, in FE, vocational teachers may see their role as preparing their students to work in the world rather than just teaching a subject, whereas a teacher in a school may see themselves as a teacher of geography or history, etc., and this influences the way that they work with their students and the way that society sees them. The field of special students is a small part of the larger field of FE. This will affect the way that the sub-field and those who work or learn within it are seen by those in the larger field. From the conversation above you can see that the students in the PMLD/MLD field are not fully included within the bigger field of the college. The fence that surrounds this sub-field, although well-intentioned and designed to protect those within it, has the potential to a create *a 'ghetto' of students with more complex difficulties with no real part to play in the sort of … [inclusive] … society … [the college] … envisages* (Dyson, 2001, p 28).

In organising the students as a separate and distinctive group you can see that the institution exercises considerable power in relation to the physical presence of these students within the college. Both Foucault and Bourdieu wrote extensively on the concept of power and its use within society in the regulation of the individual. In addition to physical power relationships, both recognised the substantial influence on groups and individuals of the hidden discourses or habituses which control the views of a society and govern the nature and type of inclusion that is possible within the FE environment.

Capitals and access to society

One of the concepts most associated with the work of Bourdieu (1993, in O'Brien and Ó Fathaigh, 2005) is the idea of different forms of 'capital'. By capital he meant things that an individual can gain and are valued by society. He identified four main types of capital:

- *economic capital*, which is largely associated with material wealth;

- *social capital*, the network of social relations or contacts developed by an individual;

- *cultural capital*, the products of education, which can be such things as vocabulary, speech patterns or qualifications, or even the *caché* attached to an individual by their having attended a particular institution; and

- *symbolic capital*, which refers to the symbols associated with other forms of capital – graduation ceremonies for cultural capital, money for economic capital or influential friends (or perhaps these days even the number of 'friends' on social media sites) for social capital.

As a teacher in FE I'm sure that you try to ensure that all your students increase their capital in each of these areas and you can probably think of lots of examples from your own practice of your students gaining one form of capital or another.

Some students are more able to access the different forms of capital than others. For example, those following higher-level qualifications may find it easier to access cultural and symbolic capital than those following entry-level courses. In order to assess our students' level of access to capitals, we need to look at three other forms of social capital which build on the work of Bourdieu: *bridging and bonding capitals* identified by Putnam (2000, pp 22–3) and *linking capital* identified by Woolcock (2001, p 13). Bonding capital is best described as the social networking between family or friendship groups that share similar characteristics. The shared interests of these groups not only support the collective interests of all the members but can also act as a safety net for marginalised individuals such as those with PMLD or MLD by caring for them and helping them to access society. Bridging capital, by contrast, refers to the social networks that exist between diverse groups such as work-based groups, which allow information (or gossip!) to move between one group and another. For example, one person might know about a job vacancy and pass the information on to another member of the group. Linking capital is slightly different in that it is characterised by relationships between individuals or groups with different levels of power. By using connections with more powerful groups or individuals, members of less powerful groups are able to access a wider range of resources and relationships than are available through bonding or bridging groups. In education, for example, careers officers have a high degree of linking capital in that they are able to make contact with universities and colleges or with employers to enquire about employment prospects on behalf of students.

All of these forms of capital can be accessed by individuals at some level, but some can access them more easily than others. Our special students are able to access only limited amounts of capital on their own, but their access to capital can be increased depending on the way that they are 'managed' by the college. The ways that FE acts to facilitate increased access to capital for special students can reflect the type and nature of inclusive practices within the institution.

CASE STUDY

The special student's view

Jessie is one of the more active and able MLD students at a college of FE. She transferred to the college from a local special school at 16 and is now in her second year in the First Level Learning area, having been awarded the Student of the Year trophy for the curriculum area at the end of her first year. She has been assessed for Disability Living Allowance (DLA) and she now lives in a supported environment in sheltered accommodation. As she is coming towards the end of her course she has been talking to one of the careers advisers at the college about her next steps.

Adviser: *What sort of things do you learn at college, Jessie?*

Jessie: *I work in the shop at college. It's part of my course. I like working in the shop. I work in the café too. And I help in the garden. And I do lessons.*

Adviser: *What sort of things do you learn, Jessie?*

Jessie: *I need to smile at customers. I need to put money in the till and give a receipt when I sell something. And I need to say 'Thank you. Please come again.'*

Adviser: *Can you do all that by yourself?*

Jessie: *No, Shelley does it with me or I give the wrong money back. And I ask people what they want to order; but Shelley writes it down.*

Adviser: *What do you do in your lessons?*

Jessie: *I do colouring and copying. And I learn numbers and money and we do shapes. And I do my letters. And I'm making the angel for the Christmas tree. Shelley cut out the bits and I stick them down. I do cooking too. Shelley writes it down in my book. And we went on a trip to see a play. And I use a computer to write things and to make things. And I look things up on the internet.*

Adviser: *Do you do all your lessons in the same place?*

Jessie: *Yes. In our classroom, ... and in the other place.*

Adviser: *Do you join in with other students in the college, Jessie?*

Jessie: No. We have our own teachers. We have dinner with them in the refectory but I don't talk to them. I sit with my friends and Shelley.

Adviser: And what do you want to do when you leave college?

Jessie: I don't want to leave. I'm going to stay here and help Shelley.

Critical thinking activity: reading between the lines

Re-read the conversation between the tutor and the student in the first critical thinking activity (pp 97–98) and then read the conversation between Jessie and the careers adviser above again. Consider the following questions.

» *What types of social capital is Jessie able to access?*

» *What level of access to social capital does she have?*

» *How have the arrangements that the college has made for the PMLD and MLD students influenced their access to different forms of capital?*

» *How inclusive do you think the college is?*

Linking to capital

Having read the case study you will have noticed that Jessie is able to access different amounts of the various forms of capital. She has her own money (DLA) and handles money in her 'work' (economic capital); she has formed a friendship group with whom she lunches (social capital); she was the Student of the Year for her area (cultural capital); and was awarded a personal trophy that represents her effort and achievement (symbolic capital). However, Jessie's access to capital lies within the curriculum area and is gained within the heavily supported environment of the sub-field. In order to gauge her level of inclusion within the wider field we need to know whether her access to this limited form of capital facilitates inclusion within the college as a whole.

In terms of gaining employment, bridging capital is frequently of more use to individuals than bonding capital, especially for special students who may well need to access informal networks to obtain work on a paid or voluntary basis. For bridging and linking capitals to be developed, students require opportunities to access the wider field of education; but you will have noticed from the case study that Jessie's opportunity to access these is limited. Her ability to use bonding capital is limited to her immediate social group and she has limited access to the wider society of the college. Given that one of the acknowledged roles of FE is the preparation of students to be included within society, you might like to think about whether the level of bonding capital which Jessie experiences within her area can compensate for the lack of bridging and linking capitals apparently available to her.

Learning the rules

In the case study you will have seen that Jessie talks very proudly about the 'work' that she does both in class and as a form of work experience. You might feel that the culture of the college in working with students like Jessie to develop their social, work and academic skills mirrors the opportunities that are offered to mainstream students. Like mainstream students she learns practical skills in addition to academic skills. Like mainstream vocational students she has the opportunity to achieve an increased level of independence and self-esteem through work experience, and life skills through interaction with other people in the college enterprises. However, from her description of the activities which she carries out it is clear that she is heavily and consistently supported to achieve these objectives. In both areas of her 'work' she receives equally high levels of support while following a bespoke curriculum which concentrates on functional and life skills.

Disciplinary power and inclusion

After reading both the case studies you may have formed a very positive opinion about the steps the college is taking to ensure that Jessie is learning the knowledge and communication skills that will enable her to be included within society. However, Foucault would see such activities as an example of *disciplinary power* being used to control the individual. Disciplinary power is self-regulating in that each individual internalises the normative rules and patterns of behaviour which apply to particular situations. Once an individual has learned the 'rules' of the context, they discipline themselves to behave in the way society expects. By using the timetables which *establish rhythms, impose particular occupations ... [and] ... regulate the cycles of repetition* (Foucault, 1991: 149) that Jessie follows, Foucault suggests that what FE is doing is producing students who are simply able to conform to the expectations of society.

Critical thinking activity: inclusion or conformity?

The college has obviously taken steps to try to prepare students with MLD and PMLD for inclusion within society by developing enterprises in which they can learn new skills and interact with people outside their normal group. Re-read the conversation between Jessie and the careers adviser.

» *How useful do you feel that this approach is in developing their bridging capital?*

» *Is the college taking positive steps to promote inclusion or is it training special students to conform?*

The pressure for conformity

Due to the nature of their physical, mental, emotional or behavioural difficulties, special students find it difficult to conform to society's expectations. You might want to argue that by creating opportunities for them to gain social and workplace skills the college is investing heavily to add to the special students' personal human capital so that they can be more fully included in the society of the college and eventually society as a whole. However, noting the relative powerlessness of special students like Jessie, Bourdieu and Foucault would analyse the situation in a different way. For them the role of FE would be to ensure her unquestioning acceptance of the rules of the 'game', the prevailing values and behaviours of the field (in this case the vocational workplace and the college) in order for her to be included within it. If you read Jessie's answers again you may gain the impression that she is simply being coached to understand her own place in relation to others.

Informal control

Both Foucault (through his concept of disciplinary power) and Bourdieu (through his analysis of the influence of habitus) recognise the pressures on the individual to conform to social norms. As was discussed in chapter 2, the concept of norms – the standards against which members of society are judged – is a critical notion when examining inclusion or inclusive practices, because norms are the measures used to determine who should be included or excluded and why. However, in addition to this subtle form of manipulation of the individual to conform to the prevailing gaze, Foucault also explored more direct methods of social control through the notion of *surveillance*.

Inclusion or control?

CASE STUDY

The teacher's view

It's hard, you know, this job. Other teachers think that because we work with students that are different and use different sorts of sensory learning with them that we don't actually teach them anything, we just play with them. They look down on us even though we've got the same qualifications as them, because they think this is an easy job that anyone could do – just babysitting really and you don't need to be a qualified teacher to do that do you? They don't see that you're not just responsible for teaching them the 'academic' stuff but you teach them how to communicate and talk to people and behave, how to belong to society even in a small way, but that needs a lot of time, effort and patience. They have good days but they also have bad days, and when they have a bad day it really takes it out of you emotionally as well as physically. It's like being hit by a whirlwind. You know that there's something wrong but they can't always tell you what it is right away and everything you have planned for them has to be put on hold until you have sorted out whatever it is that's got them into a state.

We do what we can really. We have to try to get them through qualifications now because that's what the government says, but is that really the best thing for them? They are different. They're not like mainstream students who can help themselves – they need help all the time even with the stuff we take for granted. When I first came here I was helping out with all sorts of people who needed a bit of support and we did life skills with them, you know, cooking and budgeting and shopping and so on to help them become more independent. I think that was really useful. A lot of them can't do that much on their own, but every step towards becoming a bit more independent and doing things without help was a milestone and it made us all feel as though we had achieved something. We've got some really good facilities here for them. There's the shop and the café and the garden in the summer and they can mix with the public. The college has also invested in some really good classrooms in the main building for the more disadvantaged students, with better facilities so that we can take care of their personal needs. And that's as well as the facilities for the MLD students we have in the other building. But now, well now we have to get them to do more academic work and make sure they work towards academic targets; we still work with them on their independence skills, but it's becoming more difficult, a bit more of a balancing act in some respects.

We try to help the more able ones get some sort of work even if it's just voluntary work in one of the charity shops for a few hours a week. But in reality quite a lot of them will just disappear into the system when they leave here. I suppose quite a lot of them will just live on benefits; some of them may get little flats and be able to live in some sort of supported living environment, but we don't really know what happens to them when they leave us and that worries me. You build up trusting relationships with some of the students and they really talk to you, and they sort of become a family while they are here, even helping each other sometimes.

Critical thinking activity: perceptions of inclusion

Think about the teacher's view of her role in the inclusion of special students.

» *How does she see her role?*

» *How does she think that others see her role?*

Perspectives and perceptions of inclusion

As you will know from your own experience of working in FE, special students have already been judged by society to deviate from the norm physically, mentally or emotionally. The processes of identifying, categorising and labelling individuals with special needs which has to be carried out in FE in order to access funding makes their differences even more visible, recognisable both to themselves (in some instances) and to others. All members of an institution are subject to its controls (the formal rules and informal norms of behaviour within the institution); and their position in the society of the institution (in this case the college) is dictated by the institution itself. FE, like all institutions, tends to favour those students who are able to conform to the prevailing norms, whilst others, such as those with special needs, are placed at a disadvantage.

In your notes you will probably have jotted down that Jessie's teacher, Kate, sees her own role as that of a committed teacher who is helping her students to learn the rules of society and facilitating their entry into wider society in a safe and supported environment. This is particularly the case in the café and shop. The college has made a clear commitment to a social model of inclusion and people coming into these enterprises are both aware and tolerant of the challenges the students face. In all of her activities Jessie and her fellow students are systematically supported to achieve their learning objectives.

Foucault would interpret the teacher's role differently. For him the teacher is part of a *surveillance* system which checks and monitors the behaviours of students like Jessie in order to control them – to ensure that they conform so that they can be integrated rather than included in society. Looking back to the conversation between Jessie and the careers adviser it is clear that in this view surveillance extends beyond the monitoring of behaviour and progress towards formal educational targets. Foucault would also argue that the informal social interactions of special students with mainstream students, in the time they spend in the refectory for example, is subject to surveillance as they sit with their LSAs whose role is to monitor them. Jessie's teacher is willing to set aside formal educational activities to *sort out whatever it is that's got them into a state* when required, seeing this as a positive action which is part of her duty of care for the student. But Foucault would again see this as a mechanism of surveillance.

Care or control?

From reading the teacher's comments you will have seen that she is very conscious that the students she works with are different from the norm and can be physically, mentally and emotionally challenging. You may agree with her view of her role that she is a caring person working in the best interests of the student. She is obviously committed to her work and takes pride in the steps towards independence that students make in their 'work' activities. She also ensures that, although the teaching staff are now called on to work with students to achieve qualifications, the life skills element remains a central component in her students' curriculum. She consistently observes and mentors her charges, helping them to conform to the standards required academically and socially, and regards this as part of her duty of care for the student.

However, Foucault interprets such observation and intervention by the teacher as an extension of the institution's disciplinary control over the individual, suggesting that the teacher and LSAs are an integral part of a surveillance system designed to ensure compliance rather than inclusion. The teacher's success in enabling the students to control their behaviour and function within the bounds of normative behaviour is a sign that they have been able to implement disciplinary power effectively.

Critical thinking activity: areas of conflict

Review the positions of the institution, teacher and the student in terms of inclusion.

» *Is there a commitment to inclusion and if so on what basis – segregation, integration or inclusion?*

» *Are there any areas of conflict or agreement over the way in which the role of the teacher of the special students is viewed by the teacher and the institution?*

»   *Are there areas of conflict and comparison between the types of capital that the institution and the teacher want to develop within the students?*

Views on the inclusion agenda

From your reading, and by answering the questions in this critical thinking activity, you may have come to the conclusion that in this example the institution has a commitment to inclusion but has chosen, possibly for purely practical and logistical reasons, to include these special students on a segregated basis. Although they have discrete learning locations, you will have noted the positive attempts made by the college to integrate them into the wider life of the college. In analysing the teacher's comments you will probably have decided that she feels she is working towards a wider agenda with a broader definition of inclusion. You may feel that she sees her role as preparing her students for inclusion within society by helping them to access a degree of social and economic capital by learning emotional, social and work skills. However, you may also have noticed a contradiction in her comments. Although she places considerable value on the work that she does with the special students, she places her personal value as a teacher towards the bottom of the hierarchy of teachers. There is an argument, however, that the work of the special needs teacher is of critical importance in developing the art of teaching itself. As Norwich and Lewis (2001) note, many of the approaches initially used within a special education context now inform mainstream teaching and learning. The knowledge of the special needs area, in terms of its use of inclusive activities, resources and teaching methods, is increasingly being transferred into the mainstream provision and challenging the consecrated knowledge of vocational education in FE.

Conclusion

The position of special students in FE is one that is contentious and unstable, and is primarily defined by the gaze of the individual institution. Competing agendas of control, inclusion, differentiation and access have fragmented the approach of FE to the education of special students and many of these students, who cannot be readily accommodated in mainstream education, risk becoming increasingly isolated within FE institutions. The training of teachers to cope with special students within the FE sector has been limited, but in 2013 for the first time, within the discipline of Initial Teacher Education there is a bespoke pathway for those who wish to work specifically within this field. Perhaps a small light has begun to signify the end of the dark tunnel, leading to the successful inclusion of this group within FE?

Chapter reflections

»   *There is no single analysis to explain the role of FE in relation to special students.*

»   *The gaze or habitus of the institution is critical in determining the position of special students in an educational setting.*

»   *The individual institution exercises considerable influence over the degree of inclusion of special students in education and eventually in society.*

»   *All students are special; some of them just have more 'specialised' needs than others.*

Taking it further

Norwich, B and Lewis, A (2001) Mapping a Pedagogy for Special Educational Needs. *British Educational Research Journal*, 27(3): 313–29.

A useful article that shows the overlap between the pedagogy of special needs and mainstream education.

Peart, S (2014) *Equality and Diversity in Further Education*. Northwich: Critical Publishing.

Includes an excellent chapter looking at international and national perspectives of disability in Further Education.

Riddell, S, Baron, S and Wilson, A (2001) *The Learning Society and People with Learning Difficulties*. Bristol: Policy Press.

A useful review of a range of policy fields and agencies involved in the delivery of services to those with learning difficulties. Interesting and descriptive narratives of the experience of individuals with learning difficulties in a lifelong learning context.

References

Allan, J (1996) Foucault and Special Educational Needs: A 'Box of Tools' for Analysing Children's Experiences of Mainstreaming. *Disability & Society*, 11(2): 219–34.

Bourdieu, P (1993) *The Field of Cultural Production*. Cambridge, UK: Polity Press.

DiGiorgio, C (2009) Application of Bourdieuian Theory to the Inclusion of Students with Learning/ Physical Challenges in Multi Cultural Schools Settings. *International Journal Of Inclusive Education*, 13(2): 179–94.

Dyson, A (2001) Special Needs in the 21st Century: Where We've Been and Where We're Going. *British Journal of Special Education*, 28(1): 24–28.

Foucault, M (1991) *Discipline and Punish: The Birth of the Prison*. London: Penguin Books.

Grenfell, M and James, D (1998) *Bourdieu and Education*. London: Falmer Press.

Hodkinson, P (1998) Career Decision Making and the Transition from School to Work, in Grenfell, M and James, D *Bourdieu and Education: Acts of Practical Theory*. London: Falmer Press.

Norwich, B and Lewis, A (2001) Mapping a Pedagogy for Special Educational Needs. *British Educational Research Journal*, 27(3): 313–29.

O'Brien, S and Ó Fathaigh, M (2005) Bringing in Bourdieu's Theory of Social Capital: Renewing Learning Partnership Approaches to Social Inclusion. *Irish Educational Studies*, 24(1): 65–76.

Orwell, G (2000) *Animal Farm*. London: Penguin Classics.

Putnam, R (2000) *Bowling Alone: The Collapse and Revival of American Community*. New York: Simon & Schuster.

Riddell, S, Baron, S and Wilson, A (2001) *The Learning Society and People with Learning Difficulties*. Bristol: Policy Press.

Watson, C (2010) Educational Policy in Scotland: Inclusion and the Controls Society Discourse. *Studies in the Cultural Politics of Education*, 31(1): 93–104.

Webb, J, Schiranto, T and Danaher, G (2002) *Understanding Bourdieu*. London: Sage.

Woolcock, M (2001) The Place of Social Capital in Understanding Economic Outcomes. *Isuma: Canadian Journal of Policy Research*, 2:(1): 1–17.

Websites

James, D (2011) *Beginning with Bourdieu in Educational Research*. British Educational Research Association. Available at www.bera.ac.uk/wp-content/uploads/2014/03/Beginning-with-Bourdieu-in-educational-research.pdf.

O'Farrell, C (2007) *Key Concepts*. Available at www.michel-foucault.com/concepts/index.html.

9 The distraction of dyslexia

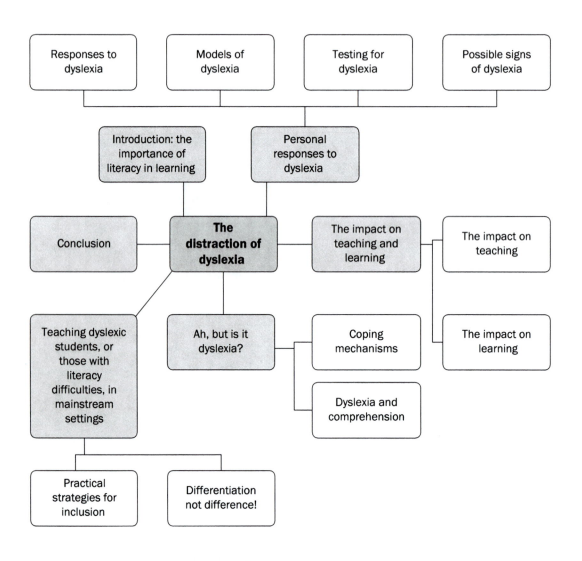

Chapter aims

This chapter sets out to help you to explore the subject of dyslexia and literacy difficulties which you will almost certainly encounter amongst the students you work with as a teacher in FE. While dyslexia is something for which there is currently no 'cure', there are ways that you as a teacher can help students with dyslexia to learn more effectively. This chapter will give you a little more information about dyslexia, the challenges that it presents to both teachers and students, and some suggestions for including students with dyslexia in mainstream learning activities.

Introduction: the importance of literacy in learning

I don't remember actually learning to read – I just assumed that as all the grown-ups I knew read books or papers it was one of those things that you could do when you were older, like being able to catch a ball or swim. My parents and immediate family all read so I copied them; they wrote letters and lists so I scribbled in imitation; they read to me so I read to them. It never occurred to me that you actually had to *learn* to read and write, or that it might be a difficult thing to do. For me it was part of growing up – adults could read and write, so I would be able to as well.

It wasn't until I went to primary school that I found out that some children didn't read as well as others. I was classed as a 'good reader' from quite an early age. Every morning the teacher would send me to sit with a group of my peers to listen to them read aloud and to help them sound out the words they found difficult. I was about seven at the time, and whilst this may well have been a very early example of the twin pedagogic practices of peer mentoring and phonics in practice, it is far more likely that it was the result of an experienced teacher, faced with a class of 35 children, using her 'resources' effectively. Whatever the reason, I rapidly learned that not only did some children need help in learning to read, but there were advantages to being able to read well. I could choose my books rather than having to read 'boring' ones with simple stories in which the same words were endlessly repeated; so I was experiencing what Tanner (2009, p 785) saw as *society ... reward[ing] its members who can read and write*.

Literacy forms the basis of our educational system and reading enables us to learn the information and knowledge which society sees as being important. In FE, as in most areas of education, we still largely test this knowledge through examinations which rely on the ability to read and/or write. Passing these examinations is important to our students as it gives them symbolic capital (a certificate) which shows that they have gained the knowledge or skills that employers want. The written exam system favours students who have no difficulty with reading or writing, but it can seriously disadvantage those who have difficulties with literacy such as dyslexia. Although it is estimated that the number of people in the general population who have difficulty with literacy is 5–10 per cent, your experience in FE may lead you to think that the number is higher than this. According to the dyslexia specialist in my college, 25–30 per cent of the students who come to us every year need support with literacy. My college is fairly typical of the sector, so these numbers suggest that virtually every teacher in FE will at any time have one or more students in their class who have literacy difficulties. You may already be working with young adults and more mature students who have 'failed' in compulsory education because of this and have come into FE to learn vocational or professional skills that utilise their other talents.

The trouble is that all of the vocational qualifications that you teach will need your students to read or write at some point and very few of us have experience in helping students with these skills. However, as Rose (2009, pp 15–16) suggests, *The quality of an education system cannot exceed the quality of its teachers ... In other words, success ... [for students] ... first and foremost depends on teachers*, so to do the best for your students you need to understand their difficulties and help them to overcome them. This isn't to say that you have to become a literacy specialist, but if you understand a little more about the difficulties that your students face with reading and/or writing you will be better able to help them. You may have already found that working with students who have literacy difficulties can be challenging (and even scary for new teachers), so the purpose of this chapter is to enable you to explore literacy difficulties and give some practical suggestions for use in the classroom.

Critical thinking activity

Think about your own experience of learning to read.

» *Did you find it easy or difficult to learn to read?*

» *Did you find things like spelling, doing 'joined up' (cursive) writing, deciphering new words or understanding and remembering new vocabulary challenging?*

» *Do you think your personal experience has affected the way in which you work with students with literacy difficulties or dyslexia/dyslexic tendencies in the classroom?*

Understanding your personal experience of reading and writing is important. Your experience of learning to read and write can influence the way that you see literacy difficulties in your students and affect the way you work in the classroom. Read the extract from Lizzie's professional development journal below. Write down the different attitudes towards literacy difficulties held by those involved and the impact that dyslexia may have on including students in the learning process.

Personal responses to dyslexia

CASE STUDY

'Stuff' – a first experience of dyslexia

Entry 1: discovery!

Well today was interesting. My first day with an established group of students working towards level 2 in basic skills as part of their vocational programme in business studies I was 'picking up' from a colleague about to go on maternity leave. In they all trooped; fourteen of them, eleven boys and three girls, complete with earphones, mobile phones and 'attitude'. After the introductions, explanations and their moans and groans about having to do functional skills which they could not see the point of (quelle suprise!!) I got them working on drafting letters to meet the criteria they had been working on with my erstwhile colleague, while I started to see each of them with their files.

'Stuff' – that was the only word one student uttered as he tipped his file of work onto my desk when I asked to see his folder. 'Don't worry Miss,' chipped in his friend (his only friend as I later discovered), as I gazed in disbelief at the unruly heap of papers. 'He don't talk much and his file is always like this – just "stuff".' On examination 'stuff' pretty well summed it up; no logic, no order, no organisation, simply the detritus from any and every class he had attended. Dutifully handed to whoever asked to see it, it was, I suspect, something that was hastily handed back to its owner after a cursory glance at the chaos it contained.

At break I found my colleague and asked for some guidance, or at least an insight into his situation and work. 'Don't worry about him,' was all she said. 'He's supposed to be dyslexic but I think he's just lazy, and a bit thick. He's not going to pass the course anyway. He can barely read and his writing – no hope; can't spell, no idea about grammar, so, well, ... just forget about him, keep him occupied and he won't be any trouble. Let him play on the internet and find music – he's quite good at that.'

I have worked in Youth Training (YT) for long enough to be used to the challenge of supporting and working with young people who have dropped out of education, have poor literacy skills, are behaviourally challenging, who regard themselves as failures with no prospects and who feel that they have been 'written off' by society as 'ne'er do wells' by the age of sixteen. But I'm working in a college now, in FE. I'm an educator amongst educators, part of an institution dedicated to learning and development. I'm supposed to be helping him to learn, so how can I just 'forget about him', and what is dyslexia anyway? HELP!!!

Entry 2: the harsh reality

OK – having been down and talked to 'Support' it appears that it is 'too late' to arrange for him to be assessed as he has been here for 18 months and is due to complete at the end of the academic year. In effect, if I think he needs support it's going to be down to me to provide it. Well, I'm no specialist but someone's got to help him. But where on earth do I start?

Responses to dyslexia

You will probably have noted two very different responses to students with dyslexia in this vignette. On the one hand there is the teacher who appears to have written off the student and seems to think that the student's literacy difficulties are due to his laziness and lack of intelligence. The newer and less-experienced teacher is more challenged by the situation. Rather than writing off the student she wants to take responsibility for learning. She tries to find help for the student, but becomes frustrated both by the attitude of her colleagues and the difficulty of obtaining support. Her final comment – *where on earth do I start?* – is an expression of her feelings of helplessness and recognition of her own need for support in this situation.

Models of dyslexia

One of the biggest difficulties that teachers have in understanding dyslexia (and you may have already experienced this) is the lack of agreement over its nature and cause. Until recently dyslexia wasn't recognised as a specific learning difficulty and there was little research into its cause. Recent research has resulted in a continuum, or range, of explanations. At one end of the continuum are the medical models, in which dyslexia is regarded as a 'brain-based' learning disability that can be identified through formal assessments; at the other end are the social models that see dyslexia as a personal difficulty which can be overcome, or at least made less of a challenge, through the right support.

The medical models see dyslexia as an inborn 'learning difficulty' (International Dyslexia Association, 2008), something that individuals are born with and which will affect them throughout their lives. Vellutino et al. (2004) and Goswami (2008) see dyslexia as a processing difficulty within the brain which can affect the development of individuals' ability to link phonemes together to make up words. (Phenomes are the sounds that make up words – cat has three distinct sounds 'c' 'a' and 't'.) This could also lead to other difficulties in understanding the semantics and orthography (the meaning and spelling of words) of language. Tests have been developed to assess these difficulties in students who may have dyslexia or dyslexic tendencies – the difficulties in reading or writing associated with dyslexia which you will explore later in this chapter. Some of your students may have been tested already. If they have, then your students' results can be compared to 'normal' results and areas of difficulty identified which could be addressed through specific training or 'interventions' by either yourself or specialists. This is very much a *deficit* model of disability as your students are tested to see if there is something 'wrong' with them and it concentrates on what the student *can't* do rather than what they *can* do in terms of literacy.

The medical model can be criticised for not taking account of external factors which influence literacy development. Individual circumstances such as the home background of your students; their access to books; whether education is seen as important by their family; or cultural factors (eg English might be a student's second language) can all affect literacy. Social influences are something that you will take into account when working with any student, but it is particularly important for you to think about them when working with students who have literacy difficulties. Social models of dyslexia take these into account and suggest that instead of (or sometimes as well as) using 'interventions', you and your colleagues can help students by making your classrooms more dyslexia friendly. By introducing enabling arrangements – activities and resources which enable students with literacy difficulties to take part in the learning process – you will be able to help them to *demonstrate their strengths and abilities and show attainment* (Reid, 2009, p 8) in the classroom. For example, you might think about a group activity using an online noticeboard. This will not only let students with dyslexia use computers to write and spell-check their work, but it also lets them research using screen-reading functions which are built into many computers, tablets and smartphones – fun activities that they will enjoy. In this model dyslexia is not seen as a difficulty within the individual but a challenge for the society of the classroom, a problem for inclusive practice rather than a statement of need for exclusion.

Possible signs of dyslexia

At the present time there is no single definition of dyslexia. The one that is currently most influential in FE is that given in the Rose Report (2009, pp 9–10) which defines it as *a learning difficulty that primarily affects the skills involved in accurate and fluent word reading and spelling*. Although it is most commonly associated with word recognition and spelling difficulties, dyslexia can also reveal itself in other ways. Perhaps you have experience of some of those listed below:

- auditory difficulties: difficulty in recognising or repeating sounds in words;
- visual difficulties: not recognising letters or being able to discriminate between visually similar letters ('b' and 'd' or 'p' and 'q', for example);
- organisational difficulties: ordering tasks or structuring writing;
- sequencing difficulties: confusing the order of letters, words or digits;
- memory difficulties: inability to follow instructions, particularly when a list of instructions is given all at once;
- motor difficulties: poor co-ordination, doing simple tasks simultaneously, clumsiness.

A word of warning

While all of these characteristics may indicate dyslexia, you will recognise that they are also signs of other learning difficulties such as speech, hearing, vision or developmental disorders such as attention deficit hyperactivity disorder (ADHD). Current research shows that about half of those who have dyslexia also experience co-morbidity (have other learning difficulties in addition to dyslexia) and this may well be the case with some students you have encountered.

Testing for dyslexia

Given the range of possible indicators, you will see that identifying dyslexia can be fraught with difficulties (so difficult sometimes that a colleague specialising in dyslexia describes it as *something of a dark art*). Assessment for dyslexia is outside the scope of this chapter, but you should note when reading about the subject that different strategies may be recommended for different age groups. Young children may require additional support to develop phonic awareness to give a firm foundation for the later development of literacy skills. However, older or more experienced readers such as those that you work with may have already developed these skills to some degree and have difficulty in comprehension and understanding rather than just reading words. Assessment for dyslexia needs to be matched to the needs of the student and the particular difficulties that they may be experiencing, and it must be as individual as the student who is being considered.

Critical thinking activity

Imagine a scenario where one of your students is dyslexic or has literacy difficulties.

»   *What do you do to try to help them?*

»   *Does the help you give come from a medical or social approach (or possibly both)?*

»   *How do you promote the inclusion of students with literacy difficulties in your classroom?*

The impact on teaching and learning

One of the biggest problems with dyslexia is that it is not visible or easily identified but nevertheless it has a significant impact on the individual.

Critical thinking activity: causes for concern

Read the following case study and write down what you think are the causes for concern exhibited by Mary.

»   *What is the impact that being an unidentified dyslexic has had on Mary?*

»   *What impact has Mary's lack of diagnosis had on her teachers?*

»   *How has this affected inclusion in teaching and learning?*

CASE STUDY

The problem of unidentified dyslexia

Mary and her sister Jane are both taking an Access course to enable them to gain the necessary qualifications to attend university in the future. Jane, although having two small children, is coping with the course well, submitting work on time and gaining merit grades. Mary, her younger sister, is causing her tutors some concern. Her work (when she submits any) is generally late and she is frequently absent on hand-in day. There is a developing pattern of non-attendance; if Jane is unable to attend for childcare reasons, Mary rings in sick. More importantly the tutors are all beginning to worry about Mary's behaviour in class. *It's like looking at a rabbit caught in headlights* was one comment at the recent tutors' meeting; and, *In class she just doesn't seem to 'get it'. She can't answer the questions and she just backs out of discussions; she just won't communicate* was the comment from another.

In a tutorial the course leader challenged Mary about her work and during the discussion Mary told her that she had been tested for dyslexia some time ago but she had dropped out of college before being told the results. She agreed to be tested again because she was finding the reading *a bit difficult*. The results of her test, to quote the assessor, were *worryingly low*, showing her to have the reading age of an eight year old and the writing age of a six year old. *Well that explains everything then, doesn't it?* was the comment of the course leader when given the assessment results. *But how did she manage to get the grades to come on the course? She's got Cs and Ds at GCSE and the odd B as well. How did she get them if she is dyslexic? Why wasn't it picked up at school? Someone must have noticed she was struggling before she got to us. We need to get someone in from Learning Support.*

During the interview that forms part of the dyslexia assessment Mary was eventually open about her previous educational experience. As a child she had difficulties with her hearing and had missed quite a lot of school due to illnesses. She had struggled with reading *right from being in primary school* but had deflected attention from her difficulties by being *a nightmare student*, just *naughty* enough in class to be sent out, ignored by the teacher, or put in detention; but not disruptive enough to be excluded. Her teachers put her lack of progress down to behavioural difficulties and she was not assessed for dyslexia at any point during her compulsory education. For homework she had relied on Jane's help in *translating* and explaining things, and sometimes she simply resorted to copying. Her aunt was sympathetic and she e-mailed her course work to her for correction before submitting it through the Virtual Learning Environment. As all work was submitted electronically she never had to 'give in' written work and her difficulties with writing, spelling and grammar were not picked up. As a result of the coping strategies and support network that she had developed while at school, and by choosing practical rather than academic subjects for GCSE, she managed to gain some respectable results and had qualified for entry to the Access course.

The impact on teaching

Like the teachers in this cameo you may have felt frustrated when an apparently ordinary student does not make the progress you expect. But dyslexia is frequently something that is hidden. In theory, dyslexia is something that is identified and managed during compulsory education. However, you may have already met students who have chosen to hide their literacy difficulties. Because literacy difficulties can be seen as a sign of being 'stupid', some students prefer to be seen as disruptive to deflect attention from their difficulty rather than being identified as having literacy problems. How we see ourselves (our self-image) and how others see us is important to all of us, but it is especially important to students with literacy difficulties. Ferri et al. (2005) suggest that the way you, as a teacher, see dyslexia is important in how students with dyslexia see themselves. Your attitudes and actions in the classroom can reveal your preconceptions, and your students sense this. The way in which you see dyslexia and the accommodation and support you offer to students with this difficulty can be critical in the way they feel about themselves and how they feel they can progress in education.

The course leader in this case study appears to feel a sense of relief once the assessment process has 'bagged and tagged' the student's difficulty as dyslexia. For her, the label 'dyslexia' explains the student's difficulty, which she sees as a medical problem that requires specialist help. Attaching the label of dyslexia to the student has redefined the student's position in relation to learning, marking her out as different and potentially providing a reason for her to be excluded from the learning process.

The impact on learning

The way in which students view their dyslexia also varies considerably. Some students you may have met see it as a 'disability', an indication that they are deficient in some way, and may even see themselves as 'stupid'. You may have already met students whose feelings of inadequacy have led to their 'giving up'; any success that they may have they see as the result of good luck rather than something which is within their control. Other students who see their dyslexia as a barrier to learning may 'act out' or appear to be 'not bothered' or 'not interested' rather than having to face their difficulty or the embarrassment of being seen as 'different' by their peers. However, there are some students who see dyslexia as a learning *difference* rather than a disability, and they recognise both the positive and negative aspects of the condition. One of my beginning educators (who is herself dyslexic) found that by embracing the condition she accepted her 'difference' as a part of being her, allowing her as she said to *grow straight and tall* rather than hiding from the world.

Critical thinking activity

Take a few minutes to think about how you deal with students who are disruptive in your class.

»   *Are there any similarities between their behaviour and that of Mary?*

»   *Is there a possibility that their behaviour could be masking a literacy problem? How could you check?*

Ah, but is it dyslexia?

Dyslexia, as explained above, is a condition that is usually associated with a lack of fluency in reading and spelling, but it can manifest itself in subtle forms which are more difficult to recognise.

Critical thinking activity: it's not just about being able to read!

»   *Read the case study below in relation to the indicators noted above and decide whether you feel Tom exhibits signs of dyslexia/dyslexic tendencies.*

»   *Write down points for and against your conclusions.*

CASE STUDY

You're wrong – I'm not dyslexic!

But I can read – I can't be dyslexic. I've passed exams. I've got a level 3 in media studies. I'm not dyslexic. I'm just not. I can read! This was the horrified reaction of Tom, a mature student working as a technician/tutor in the media department of an FE college, when it was suggested that it might be worth exploring the possibility that he had dyslexic tendencies which could explain the difficulties he appeared to be having in coping with the written element of his level 5 DTLLS course. His work for the course up to that point had been largely narrative, showing little evidence of background reading or planning, and indicated that he was having difficulty in relating what he had read to his personal professional practice. In practical sessions, however, he had excelled, making good contributions to group discussions, confidently taking the lead in computer-based activities and ably supporting any of his colleagues who experienced technical mishaps. However, throughout the course he had ensured that he was not called upon to write or take notes in group activities, using his poor writing and left-handedness as excuses for devolving this task to others.

The following is part of the referral form submitted to request a dyslexia assessment for Tom. His tutors and mentor had become increasingly concerned by his underperformance in the theory/written component of the course, which did not seem to match his practical ability.

Does XXX have difficulties with any of the following?	yes	no
Completing tasks in class lessons	✓	
Running out of time in exams	NA	
Writing speed	✓	
Legibility of work	✓	
Spelling	✓	
The length of his/her work compared to peers	✓	
Answering the exact question set	✓	
Producing written work	✓	
Written work matching his/her verbal ability	✓	
Underperforming under time conditions	NA	
Understanding and/or following instructions	NA	
Handing in assignments or other work on time	✓	
Concentration in class	✓	

Other (please list details below)

He is currently being supported to achieve on his DTLLS course through regular one-to-one tutorials in which the underpinning theory taught in class is reiterated and made specifically relevant to his personal experience and expertise in media. Course tutors have found that diagrams, flow charts and mind maps in addition to those used in class activities are required in the tutorial situations in order to enable him to assimilate information. He uses the internet in preference to books to find information as this can be targeted through search engines, but experiences difficulty in using information he finds in this way to inform his essays and link theory with practice. In class he is happy to listen and work orally, but frequently has to have concepts and theories explained several times using a variety of formats. He is reluctant to take notes and is reliant on his knowledge of computer technology to support his academic endeavours. He uses a tablet whenever one is available to take notes rather than writing by hand. There is a considerable discrepancy between his oral contributions and his written work, which continues to be narrative, descriptive and derivative and which shows depressingly little evidence of reading or analysis to support his suppositions. His line manager informs us that his writing and spelling are also giving cause for concern when he has to hand-write comments on the work of his students.

When tested for dyslexia using the standard assessments, Tom's results indicated that his reading, word recognition, comprehension and spelling were within the low average range, although his working memory score and those scores connected with decoding skills were marginally below average. Due to his age (Tom was almost 24, which is the upper limit for reliability in the standard assessments used by the college) and the disparity between the tutors' comments and the assessment results, the assessor decided to introduce a more sophisticated comprehension test which tested working memory and recall of information rather than his ability to select appropriate words to complete sentences. This test showed a significant weakness in both his ability to remember what he had read and also in locating information in text.

Dyslexia and comprehension

As we saw earlier, there is a high percentage of students with dyslexia or dyslexic tendencies. Most of the students that you are likely to work with will have enough literacy skills to be able to read words and sentences. But the literacy skills your students need to be successful in FE require them to progress from being able to read words to skills of comprehension, analysis and evaluation of text. You may find that one or two of your students, particularly those who are studying for more advanced qualifications, struggle to write essays because although they have no problems reading words they don't remember or understand what they have read. This difficulty might be due to something called hyperlexia. The student's short-term memory, which passes information to other parts of their brain, is overloaded by the effort of reading the words so that it is unable to access the long-term memory to retrieve their meaning (something which is normally done almost simultaneously), and their comprehension suffers as a result. Unfortunately this difficulty is not always picked up by the standard tests used for testing dyslexia, most of which concentrate on reading words rather than testing understanding and comprehension.

Coping mechanisms

Tom's reaction to the suggestion that he was dyslexic is typical of many older students and this is challenging for teachers. As you will have seen when reading the case study, Tom had come into FE with a range of strategies for literacy that he uses in his work and social life. He works in media and is skilled in the use of computers, tablets and electronic devices which help him to work effectively in teaching and learning situations where their use is permitted. In this case it is unlikely that any support in reading itself is necessary and the presence of a Learning Support Assistant (LSA) might prove embarrassing to the student. For this type of student, who is fairly self-sufficient in most things, support can often be provided by the teacher through changes to the delivery pattern.

Critical thinking activity

»   *Think about the case studies on Mary and Tom that you've already looked at in this chapter and write down the type(s) of support that you feel is (or are) most appropriate to each.*

»   *Where possible, suggest strategies that could be employed for each of the students and justify your ideas by referring to the detail of the case studies.*

Teaching dyslexic students, or those with literacy difficulties, in mainstream settings

Differentiation not difference!

As we saw above, dyslexia/dyslexic tendencies are not only difficult to identify but are unique to the individual student. However good you are, you cannot 'fix' dyslexia; but you can work towards including dyslexic students in the classroom and use your teaching skills to help them learn. Support in FE is only effective if the student is willing to accept it; and as we have seen, some students, especially those whose dyslexia makes them feel inadequate as students, may reject the idea of LSA support. Teachers are wily souls and know that if they can use strategies that their students 'own' to include them in learning they can often support their students without them being aware of it. But because dyslexia is unique to the student it is clearly essential that you are fully aware of the student's individual strengths and weaknesses, previous experience, learning style and any specific concerns they may have about learning.

You may agree with Norwich and Lewis (2001) who suggest that in any group there are three different sorts of needs – those that are common to all students; those that are specific to a small group of the students; and individual needs. Although some specific strategies may need to be used to support students with dyslexia, many of these also meet the needs of non-dyslexic students who may struggle with some aspects of literacy. Based on strategies that emphasise *differentiation* not *difference*, changes to teaching practices can benefit all students; and barriers to learning and participation can be reduced so that the classroom becomes an enabling rather than a 'disabling' environment for students with dyslexia. For example, activities that actively 'scaffold' (Bruner, 1983) learning benefit most students, as does working through the Learning Cycle model developed by Kolb (1984). Advance organisers (Ausbel, 1963) which enable you to give specific, measurable, achievable, realistic and timebound (SMART) learning outcomes at the start of the teaching, inclusive strategies mini summaries, specific, contextualised information and continuous reinforcement through discussion or activities, all support students in general and dyslexic students in particular.

Practical strategies for inclusion

Presenting information

Hatcher et al. (2002) suggest that there are four main areas of concern for students with dyslexia:

*   their speed of reading and writing;

*   their ability to research information;

*   their ability to remember information;

*   their ability to use information and organise their work.

In your teaching you can address all of these points by ensuring that you present information in ways which do not overwhelm them, and making sure that key points are reinforced. Using multisensory approaches to learning – the *hear it, say it, see it and write it* method suggested by Reid (2009, p 166) – helps students to remember information. And making sure that new information is placed in a context that is familiar is another way you could help those with (and without!) dyslexia to learn.

Alternative activities

In the classroom you may already have found that peer learning, where students work together to find information, discuss findings and create mind maps or spidergrams, can be used as cues for learning groups. You can encourage students to work together to build writing frames for assignments that focus the thought processes of all students and are particularly useful for students with dyslexia. Using text-to-speech software (headphones essential!) is an exciting and inclusive way of encouraging all students to 'read' in preparation for tasks. These allow students to read and hear information simultaneously from computers and mobile devices, and they can highlight important points through the use of inexpensive apps. You probably already ask students to make posters for presentations; but if these are recorded digitally (with the permission of all participants of course) and uploaded to a VLE, they can become a reference source that can be accessed by students at home or outside college.

Individual support

Your role as a teacher in helping students with dyslexia to understand new concepts and ideas cannot be underestimated. The time you spend with your students in tutorials planning assignments and discussing ideas, although time-consuming, is immensely valued by such students. The consistent, constructive and specific feedback in which you detail their strengths and areas for development is also important. Feedback of this sort helps them to understand how they can be successful writers and enables them to gain a foothold on the virtuous spiral of success rather than experiencing the destructive and downward spiral of failure.

Critical thinking activity

» *Critically reflecting on your classroom practice, think about which of the points above you could use in your teaching. Try to provide a specific example with strategies.*

» *Plan and document a change to a lesson to ensure that students with literacy difficulties are fully included.*

Conclusion

Dyslexia is a condition that is unique to the individual and as such it is about difference. Difference in the effect that it has on the individual; difference in the way that students and teachers respond to it; and difference in the ways in which it can be tackled in the classroom. If you or your students see dyslexia as a *disability* it will become one and will have a negative impact on the learning and the student. If you and your students see dyslexia as a *difference* it can become a positive influence on teaching, inspiring creative practice in the teacher and working as a positive force for inclusion in the classroom. It's all about difference, not disability!

Chapter reflections

» *Dyslexia is an individual condition whose impact is unique to the individual.*

» *Dyslexia is frequently a hidden condition, but one that is lifelong.*

» *Different models and perspectives on dyslexia generate different responses in teachers and students, and in teaching and learning.*

» *Technology is a tool for teaching and learning which can greatly assist students with dyslexia, but it is not a solution.*

» *Strategies for working with students with dyslexia can help all students.*

» *Dyslexia is not a bar to inclusion in the classroom and can promote creativity in teaching.*

Taking it further

Reid, G (2009) *Dyslexia: A Practitioner's Handbook*. Chichester: John Wiley and Sons Ltd.

A clear and comprehensive investigation of dyslexia and its impact on teaching and learning, which contains a wealth of useful strategies for including students with dyslexia in mainstream education.

References

Ausubel, D (1963) *The Psychology of Meaningful Verbal Learning*. New York: Grune & Stratton.

Bell, S (2009) Exploring Support for Dyslexic Adults in the English Workforce: Lessons Learnt from the Story of an Adult Dyslexia Group. *Support for Learning*, 24(29): 73–80.

Bourdieu, P (1988) *Homo Academicus*. Stanford: Stanford University Press.

British Psychological Society (1999) in Reid, G (2009) *Dyslexia: A Practitioner's Handbook*. Chichester: John Wiley and Sons Ltd.

Bruner, J (1983) *Child's Talk: Learning to Use Language*. New York: Norton.

Ferri, A, Keefe, C and Gregg, N (2001) Teachers with Learning Disabilities: A View From Both Sides of the Desk. *Journal of Learning Disabilities*, 34(1): 22–32.

Ferri, B, Connor, D, Solis, S, Valle, J and Volpitta, D (2005) Ongoing Negotiations with Discourses of Disability. *Journal of Disabilities*, 38(1): 62–78.

Goswami, U (2008) Reading, Dyslexia and the Brain. *Educational Research*, 50(2): 135–48.

Hatcher, J, Snowling, M and Griffiths, Y (2002) Cognitive Assessment of Dyslexic Students in Higher Education. *British Journal of Educational Psychology*, 72: 119–33.

Humphrey, N and Mullins, P (2002) Personal Constructs and Attributions for Academic Success and Failure in Dyslexia. *British Journal of Special Education*, 29(4): 196–203.

Kolb, D A (1984) *Experimental Learning Experience as a Source of Learning and Development*. New Jersey: Prentice Hill.

Morton, J and Frith, U (1995) Causal Modelling: A Structural Approach to Developmental Psycho-pathology, in Cicchetti, D and Cohen, D. *Manual of Developmental Psychopathology*. New York: Wiley.

Norwich, B and Lewis, A (2001) Mapping a Pedagogy for Special Educational Needs. *British Educational Research Journal*, 27(3): 313–29.

Reid, G (2009) *Dyslexia: A Practitioner's Handbook*. Chichester: John Wiley and Sons Ltd.

Tanner, K (2009) Adult Dyslexia and the 'Conundrum of Failure'. *Disability and Society*, 24(6): 785–97.

Vellutino, F, Fletcher, J, Snowling, M and Scanlon, D (2004) Specific Reading Disability (Dyslexia): What have we Learned in the Past Four Decades? *Journal of Child Psychology and Psychiatry*, 45(1): 2–40.

Websites

British Dyslexia Association (2009) www.bdadyslexia.org.uk.

The International Dyslexia Association (2008) www.interdys.org.

Rose, J (2009) *Identifying and Teaching Children and Young People with Dyslexia and Literacy Difficul-ties*. London: DFCS. Available at http://webarchive.nationalarchives.gov.uk/20130401151715/https://www.education.gov.uk/publications/eOrderingDownload/00659-2009DOM-EN.pdf (last accessed on 13 February 2013).

Conclusion

Key themes

This book has looked at a variety of themes that either affect or are affected by the different understandings of what inclusion means within the FE context. Sometimes, as under the post-war Coalition government (and again under the early New Labour administrations of Blair), this challenge has been spearheaded by government policy. At other times, when the economy becomes more important than social policies, change has been forced on the sector, as you saw when the FE policies under Thatcher and Major were discussed. FE is famously flexible and has been able to change and restructure to meet the prevailing demands of different governments. Throughout all of the changes teachers have continued to work (sometimes stealthily and subversively!) to implement inclusive practice.

What has remained constant in FE, as you will perhaps have found from your own experience, is the range and disparity of young people you need to include in your teaching. Your students come from a variety of contexts and face many and often wide-ranging challenges; but many have one thing in common: they have a 'difference' which has affected their learning and prevented them from achieving their maximum potential in compulsory education. Your students' difficulties may stem from social, emotional, medical, psychological or behavioural difficulties, but each one of them wears a label of difference. This is recognised by others who then choose to include or exclude them on the basis of the preconceptions and prejudices that the label conveys to the reader. Not only do the labels of difference have a strong influence on the reader but they have a more lasting effect on the wearer, often becoming a self-fulfilling prophecy. For many of your students – SEN, NEETs or those with dyslexia, for example – the labels are negative and concentrate on what the wearer *can't* do rather than on what they *can* do; and part of your role in including these students is to challenge these labels.

The relationship that you develop with your students is critical not only in terms of helping them to learn but also in challenging negative labels. Only with your help can your students' negative feelings about themselves be dispelled and their self-esteem restored. This is a role that you may not have expected when you came into teaching in FE and one you may have found quite difficult to fulfil. The need for you to use inclusive teaching practices, group work and social learning, for example, to help your students learn more effectively is an issue that links many of the chapters. The use of such practices in terms of facilitating differentiation, engagement and motivation in a classroom form a cornerstone in the foundations of an inclusive classroom. Not only do they help the student who faces a challenge to accept (albeit slowly at times) the learning ethos, but also their peers or classmates learn to accept and work with their 'difference' – a valuable lesson for later life. Hand in glove with social learning goes the principle of differentiation, 'teaching to each', scaffolding learning through the use of inclusive activities and resources, which enable your students to access learning. By supporting your students in this way they are not only able to meet their learning objectives but also to gain a sense of empowerment, personal achievement and self-fulfilment.

It's no easy task to develop an inclusive classroom. It requires time, patience and effort, but most of all it requires understanding. Your understanding of your students, your ability to develop an empathic connection with them based on respect and acceptance (not sympathy) will encourage and invite many of them to enter education and to try again to achieve where previously they experienced only failure. Your use of your emotional intelligence, something unfortunately not covered in great depth in the current instrumental teacher education curriculum, is essential in the successful inclusion of students with labels in FE. Not all teachers find it easy to work at an emotional level and some students may need more help than they can give. In these instances the much under-praised LSA in the classroom can, where necessary and with the appropriate guidance from you, act as a mediator, not only educationally but also emotionally, between the teacher and the student.

Many themes weave their way through the fabric of this book; sometimes becoming part of the bold pattern and at other times quietly in the background, although just as important. In some respect they mirror the post-war position of FE itself, sometimes centre stage in the struggle for inclusion in education and at other times relegated to chorus, unnoticed and ignored. Nevertheless, the key players, you and other teachers within the sector, continue to play your part; and through your daily work and interactions with your students you continue to make a difference to the lives of young people, one student at a time. In the grand scheme of education this may not seem much. But to that one student who you have managed through your skills, knowledge and expertise to include in learning, the experience can be life-changing. The emphasis on inclusion remains a constant in our sector, and although its overt position in the strategic plan of the government may vary, the ethos of inclusion remains at the very heart of education within FE. At times it might seem that other priorities are more important and colleges and governments lose sight of it from time to time. But while staff continue to work in the interests of equality, inclusion will always remain the *leitmotif* of the FE sector.

Index